Contents

KV-590-692

Section Two

Introduction to the Internet
for Education

Daniel J. Kurland
Richard M. Sharp
Vicki F. Sharp

Wadsworth Publishing Company

I(T)P® An International Thomson Publishing Company

Belmont, CA • Albany, NY • Bonn • Boston • Cincinnati • Detroit • Johannesburg • London
Madrid • Melbourne • Mexico City • New York • Paris • Singapore • Tokyo • Toronto • Washington

Page Composition: Margarite Reynolds

For more information, contact Wadsworth Publishing Company,
10 Davis Drive, Belmont, CA 94002, or electronically at
http://www.thomson.com/wadsworth.html

International Thomson Publishing Europe
Berkshire House 168-173
High Holborn
London, WC1V 7AA, England

International Thomson Editores
Campos Eliseos 385, Piso 7
Col. Polanco
11560 México D.F. México

Thomas Nelson Australia
102 Dodds Street
South Melbourne 3205
Victoria, Australia

International Thomson Publishing Asia
221 Henderson Road
#05-10 Henderson Building
Singapore 0315

Nelson Canada
1120 Birchmount Road
Scarborough, Ontario
Canada M1K 5G4

International Thomson Publishing Japan
Hirakawacho Kyowa Building, 3F
2-2-1 Hirakawacho
Chiyoda-ku, Tokyo 102, Japan

International Thomson Publishing GmbH
Königswinterer Strasse 418
53227 Bonn, Germany

International Thomson Publishing
Southern Africa
Building 18, Constantia Park
240 Old Pretoria Road
Halfway House, 1685 South Africa

ISBN 0-534-52715-9

Preface

This guide is designed to meet the needs of college students first encountering the Internet.

Section One is based on *The 'Net, the Web, and You: All You Really Need to Know About the Internet ... and a Little Bit More,* by Daniel Kurland. This section is divided into five chapters. Chapter One, "Introduction," suggests the range of Internet resources. Chapter Two, "The Basics," introduces key concepts essential to a discussion of the Internet. Chapter Three, "The Internet as Medium of Communication and Collaboration," discusses individual E-mail and various programs for broader communication dependent upon E-mail. Chapter Four, "The Internet Services," offers short descriptions of each Internet program and indicates how each is used. Chapter Five, "Research and the Internet," examines tactics and techniques for research, in general and on the Internet in particular.

Section Two introduces the student to how educators in particular can benefit from the use of the Internet. After a brief introduction in Chapter 1, exercises follow in Chapter 2 which will encourage students to become proficient in the many different dimensions and uses of the Internet. Chapter 3 consists of a handy reference listing by topic of URL sites and on-line materials relevant to the discipline of Education.

Ultimately the best way to discover the Internet is on the Internet. This book is designed to get you started, and to be your companion as you explore.

This is a work, then, both to be read at your leisure for a general understanding, and to be kept by your computer as a reference guide and handbook.

SECTION ONE

Introduction 1

THE INTERNET

The Internet has been portrayed with a variety of images. Allusions are made to road systems ("the electronic superhighway"), Star Trek adventurers ("internauts in cyberspace"), and to a world community (the "electronic global village").

Initially, the Internet might best be seen within the historical development of human communication. At heart, the Internet is merely a new stage in humanity's ongoing attempt to meet people, exchange information, and explore the world of ideas. But it is also more than this.

The Internet is at once a mailbox, a research tool, a vehicle of commerce, and a medium of entertainment. You can send a letter to a colleague in Japan, check the score of the last Bullets game and the progress of a Senate bill, order a present for Aunt Harriet's birthday, listen to a sample track from a new CD, and find a recipe using avocados for supper tonight.

THE INTERNET AND THE COLLEGE STUDENT

Public discussion focuses on the Internet as a burgeoning electronic mall for cyber–consumerism and multimedia entertainment. For students and professors, the Internet has other purposes.

The Internet offers a broad array of academic and academic-related resources:

- professional and governmental archives and databases
- on-line journals
- access to commercial databases and abstract services
- professional discussion via newsgroups, mailing lists, and discussion groups
- academic and public library catalogs
- grant listings and deadlines
- directories of researchers and research projects funded by the federal government
- conference announcements and calls for papers
- academic, government and industry job announcements
- faculty biographies and university course descriptions
- educational and other software

In a broader vein, you can find the latest ferry schedule for Martha's Vineyard, browse advertisements for rafting trips, and download guides to doing your taxes.

Professors have used E–mail to post answer keys and grades, Gopher servers to archive lecture notes, and the World Wide Web to offer problem sets, interactive demonstrations, and supplementary course materials.

For graduate students and researchers, then, the Internet is an important resource for communicating with the community of scholars, for accessing sophisticated databases, for sharing information, and for investigating potential teaching/research programs.

For the undergraduate, the initial use of the Internet may be as a tool for communicating with the professor and other students. A secondary use may be to access information and discussion of real-world applications and policy issues. If you want to learn a particular discipline, study the textbook. If you want to review government documents, or discussion on issues within that discipline, surf the Internet.

The Basics

$\mathcal{2}$

How to Get On

To obtain telephone service, you must subscribe to a telephone company. To access the Internet, you must connect to an Internet provider–a host or gateway providing an on-ramp to the Internet. When a host computer offers a specific service, it is referred to as a server in a client–server relationship.

Most colleges and universities provide some form of Internet access. At one extreme, access may be limited to specific computers in a computing center or laboratory. At the other extreme, wireless access may be available campuswide.

In general, Internet access will entail one of three options:

- direct linkage to the university network
- telephone access via modem to the university network
- telephone access via modem to a local or national commercial provider

If all else fails, Internet services are available from commercial on-line services such as American Online, Compuserve, and Prodigy. Contact your computing center to assess your options.

INTERNET ADDRESSES

Each account on the Internet is assigned a unique address. House addresses divide the world into physical regions: houses on streets, in towns, in cities. Internet addresses indicate computers on networks within networks.

Each level of the network is referred to as a domain. Thus the computer running the FTP program at the National Center for Supercomputing Applications (NCSA) at the University of Illinois at Urbana–Champaign (UIUC) has the address *ftp.ncsa.uiuc.edu*. This is the Internet way of indicating a particular computer *(ftp)* at a particular center (ncsa) within a larger university network *(uiuc)*. The final abbreviation indicates the nature of the account, here an educational institution *(edu)*.

The most common final domain extensions include

edu   educational institutions

gov   government institutions

com   businesses or Internet service providers

mil   military sites

net   administrative organizations of the Internet

org   private organizations

Foreign addresses include an additional two–letter country abbreviation at the end, e.g., *ftp.nsysu.edu.tw*, the address of the FTP program at the National Sun Yat Sen University in Taiwan.

All domain addresses have a numerical Internet Protocol (IP) address equivalent. IP addresses consist of four numbers separated by dots. The notation *141.142.20.50* is the same address as *ftp.ncsa.uiuc.edu*.

MAILING ADDRESSES

Domain addresses are equivalent to street addresses. But street addresses alone are not sufficient to designate the location of a specific individual. Many individuals may live in the same house with the same street address. Similarly, a number of users may access the Internet from the same host, and hence from the same Internet address.

For this reason, the address of an individual user consists of a username and a domain address: *user@domain*, pronounced "user at domain." The username and domain address together make up a complete Internet E–mail address.

Uniform Resource Locators (URLs)

Other than for E-mail transactions, most Internet activity involves accessing files on remote computers. Each file or directory on the Internet (that is, on a host computer connected to the Internet) can be designated by a Uniform Resource Locator (URL). URLs indicate

- the program for accessing a file,
- the address of the computer on which a file is located,
- the path to that file within the file directory of that computer, and,
- the name of the file or directory in question.

Thus URLs have the form *protocol://IP Address/file path/filename*. Consider an example:

http://www.clark.net/pub/listserv/listserv.html

The first part of the address–*http://*–specifies the means of access, here Hypertext Transfer Protocol, associated with the World Wide Web. The address immediate following the double slash–*www.clark.net*–indicates the address of the computer (server) to be accessed.

Terms following single slashes–*/pub/listserv*–indicate progressively lower subdirectories on the server. And finally a specific file name–*listserv.html*–is recognizable by the period within the name and the *.html* ending indicating HyperText Markup Language–and is, again, associated with the World Wide Web. (URLs are indicated with *italics* throughout this text.)

There are URLs for all Internet protocols (telnet, FTP, Gopher, WAIS, http) as well as for E-mail addresses, file locations, and newsgroups.

For more information on URLs, see "A Guide to URLs," *http://www.netspace.org/users/dwb/url-guide.html.*

Internet Services

As noted earlier, other than for sending and receiving mail, time spent on the Internet generally involves accessing files on other computers. Any data manipulation or real creativity is done off-line on your own machine. There is, however, a wealth of material to be accessed.

All of the materials traditionally stored in a library–photographs and phonograph records, manuscripts and government documents, newspapers and academic journals, financial reports, employment listings, oral history tapes, and recipe collections–can be stored in electronic form. "We live in a world … ," Raymond Kurzweil noted in his keynote address at the Second U.S./Canada Conference on Technology for the Blind, "in which all of our knowledge, all of our creations, all of our insights, all of our ideas, our cultural expressions–pictures, movies, art, sound, music, books, and the secret of life itself–are all being digitized, captured, and understood in sequences of ones and zeroes." And anything stored can be accessed.

The Internet offers a number of approaches to accessing stored materials:

- File transfer protocol (FTP)
- Browsing Gopher menus or World Wide Web pages
- Retrieving documents from WAIS databases

And each of these services has its own search program.

In addition, the Internet incorporates a number of services involving communication, including:

- Electronic mail (E-mail)
- Mailing lists (discussion groups and newsletter subscriptions)
- Newsgroups
- Talk and chat groups

Each of these services is examined in detail in Chapter Three. For additional materials, see the The Virtual Internet Guide (*http://www.dreamscape.com/Frankvad/internet.html*).

THE WORLD WIDE WEB: THE SERVICE OF CHOICE

In the past year, the World Wide Web has become the service of choice–if for no other reason than that it combines complex text with vivid graphics, audio, and movies. More importantly, almost all of the other services can be accessed via the Web, or at least by utilizing a Web browser. With this in mind, relevant Web sites are indicated throughout this text.

For those without Web access, all of the services discussed–including World Wide Web pages themselves–can be accessed via

E–mail. (See the reference to *Accessing the Internet by E-mail* in the section on electronic mail, page 11).

FILE FORMATS

Files on the Internet are often encoded, archived, and/or compressed.

Encoded Files

One of the most common means of file transfer is via E-mail. But E-mail files must be in plain ASCII format; neither the binary files generated by word processors nor graphic images can be sent via standard E-mail. (This is not an issue with MIME enabled E–mail or file transfer protocol.) How then can these files be transmitted?

Binary text files can be reformatted as plain ASCII text, but the display attributes (fonts, boldface, and so on) would be lost. The solution to the transmission problem involves encoding the files utilizing ASCII characters. The information necessary for the fonts and display attributes is recaptured by decoding the file back into binary format.

Files can be encoded and decoded using various protocols. Each such protocol is indicated by a file extension. Uuencode, a common format on the Internet, results in **.uue* files.

Archived Files

A number of files can be joined, packed, or archived into a single file for ease of file manipulation. The most common programs for combining files are the UNIX program tar (**.tar*), MS-DOS/Windows PKZIP/PKUNZIP, and Macintosh ZipIt (**.ZIP*) programs. Archived files must be unpacked before use. Archiving enables a number of files, or all files in a directory, to be manipulated with a single command.

Compressed Files

Files can also be compressed to shorten transmission time or to simply save storage space. Compression ratio varies with the type of file. Program files generally compress to about half their size (2:1), data files more than 5:1. The UNIX compress/uncompress program (**.Z*) is often used in conjunction with the archiver tar, resulting in files of the form *.tar.z. Some programs, such as PKZIP and ZipIt, combine archiving and compression capability.

For instructions, refer to "How to Decode and View Binary Messages" on the Usenet newsgroups *alt.binaries.pictures.d* and *new.newusers.questions* and the Frequently Asked Questions file for the newsgroup *comp.compression (http://www.cis.ohio-state.edu/hypertext/faq/usenet/compression-faq/top.html)*.

GETTING HELP

Computer education has always been a social affair. When in need of help, users ask friends or colleagues who are, generally, only one step ahead in their computer expertise.

For most students, help is as close as their computing center. Many computing centers provide handouts and offer minicourses. Guides to the use of services and software are often posted on university networks.

On-line Guides

An extensive menu of guides to all aspects of the Internet and its resources is maintained by John December (*http://www.december.com/net/tools/index.html*).

Frequently Asked Questions (FAQs)

Responses to frequently asked questions are available as FAQ files. There are FAQs for almost all aspects of Internet content and use:

alt.fan.monty-python FAQ

Anonymous FTP Frequently Asked Questions (FAQ) List

Economists' Resources on the Internet

FAQ: How to find people's E-mail addresses

How to Read Chinese Text on Usenet: FAQ for alt.chinese.text

Copies of FAQs are generally available from the relevant Usenet newsgroup, or are posted on the newsgroups *news.announce.newusers*, *news.answers*, or *news.newusers.questions*.

FAQs are also archived in various locations. Copies of all FAQs can be browsed at *http://www.cis.ohio-state.edu/hypertext/faq/usenet/FAQ-List.html* or *http://www.intac.com/FAQ.html*. For in-

structions on obtaining FAQs by E-mail, and a complete list of
Usenet FAQs, send an E-mail letter to

mail-server@rtfm.mit.edu

Leave the subject blank and include the message

send usenet/news.answers/Index

followed by the line

help

with no period or subject heading.
FAQs are always a useful starting point for investigating any
Internet topic.

RFCs and FYIs

The Internet Engineering Task Force (IETF) provides a series of
documents called Requests for Comments (RFCs) on a broad range
of Internet topics. While many are highly technical, others offer
introductions to major topics. FYIs (For Your Information), a subset
of the RFCs, are particularly useful for new users (newbies). FYIs
include FAQs and "How To" guides for the various services. FYI: 23,
Guide to Network Resource Tools (*http://www.ftp.com/techsup/
fyi/fyi23.html*) describes all of the Internet services.

An RFC search page is available on the World Wide Web at
http://ds.internic.net/ds/dspg1intdoc.html.

The Internet as Medium of Communication and Collaboration

3

ELECTRONIC MAIL (E-MAIL): THE INTERNET AS POST OFFICE

Academic research relies on the efforts of a community of scholars. Central to this effort is communication. The major use of the Internet–by scientists as well as by others–is electronic mail and a number of other communications services based on electronic mail.

E–Mail

In many ways, E-mail is truly revolutionary. E-mail travels anywhere in the world in minutes, not days. You can send a document thousands of miles for the price of the phone call to your Internet provider. When you are having trouble getting through to someone on the phone: E-mail. Can't get past a secretary? E-mail.

In other respects, little has changed. You still have to have something to say to someone, and you still have to know that person's address. There is still the excitement of discovering that you have mail– and still the nuisance of wading through junk mail.

The Internet delivery system can overcome many problems, but it is not foolproof. Lines may be down or computer systems may be out. Excessive traffic may slow access to a particular location– and even the Internet cannot surmount an incorrect address. E-mail reports back unknown addresses and problems with delivery, but regular mail is more forgiving of simple errors in addresses.

All of the services of the Internet can be accessed via E-mail– albeit often in a very limited manner. For complete instructions, see "Accessing the Internet by E-mail, Doctor Bob's Guide to Offline Internet Access." The document can be obtained by sending an E-mail letter to *mail-server@rtfm.mit.edu* with the message

send usenet/news.answers/internet-services/ access-via-email

with no final punctuation.

Using E-Mail

E-mail programs are part word processor, part mailbox, and part file organizer. With almost all you may

- list mail received and mail sent
- read or delete an item from the list of documents received
- print or save a document as a file
- store frequently used names and addresses
- automatically attach signatures at the end of letters
- send replies, with portions of the original message in the reply
- forward mail by simply readdressing it
- attach other files to mail
- send a document to any number of people at once

The final feature facilitates the postal equivalent of the traditional telephone tree and enables a number of additional services considered below.

While the standard text-interface programs (mail, pine, and elm) are not particularly user-friendly, here, as elsewhere, the command **?** or **help** will usually evoke a list of commands, regardless of the program you are using. A graphic-interface program such as Eudora (Figure 1) greatly simplifies the process.

Social Considerations

Ever resourceful, E-mail users both speed their task and qualify their remarks with acronyms such as BTW (by the way), IMHO (in my

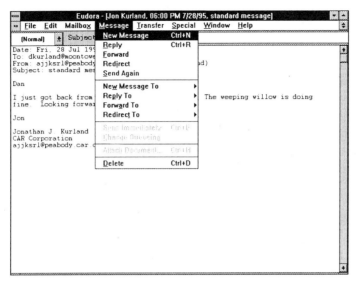

FIGURE 1 Message options on the Eudora mail program for Windows.

humble/honest opinion), FWIW (for what it's worth), and OTOH (on the other hand). Words are stressed by enclosing them in *asterisks*.

Ever playful, E-mail users have also developed a series of symbols (emoticons) to replace voice inflection and facial expressions in their letters. The most well known of these symbols is the smiley, a keyboard-written image indicating delight with an idea: :-)

Finally, users of the Internet constitute their own subculture, one that has definite standards of fair play and respect for others (netiquette). One should not YELL BY WRITING EVERYTHING IN CAPITAL LETTERS nor forward mail to large groups of people (spamming).

Sending E-mail in the privacy of your room, you might think your remarks are truly private. This is hardly the case. E-mail can be read by system administrators or your Internet provider. Mail you send to one person may be forwarded intact–or edited–to others without your knowledge or permission.

Since E-mail messages tend to be shorter than most other correspondence, you must take care not to be vague, ambiguous, or suggestive. Use sarcasm and humor cautiously to avoid misunderstandings.

Finding Addresses

Since there is no definitive Internet, there is no definitive directory of Internet names and addresses. The best way to learn a person's E-mail address is still to call the person on the telephone, or ask someone else. If that fails, you can try a number of search programs examining portions of the system. Try Four11(*http://www.four11.com*) or Yahoo's list of sites (*http://www.yahoo.com/reference/white_pages/individuals/*).

THE INTERNET AS BULLETIN BOARD, BULL SESSION, AND PARTY LINE

Mailing Lists

The same process by which a single E-mail message can be directed to another person can be used to distribute documents–almost as with traditional mailing lists.

Individuals subscribe by E-mail and receive material periodically via E-mail. (Nonsubscribers can usually request individual items from the mailing list via E-mail.) Since all such mailing list activities involve E-mail, the only software required is an E-mail program.

In many instances, subscription mailing lists are administered by a computer. The first such program was LISTSERV, giving rise to the name *listservers*. Similar programs go by the names *majordomo*, *MAILSERV*, and *listproc*.

Server computers automatically read and respond to requests to start, stop, or pause subscriptions. Most such programs oversee more than one list at a single site. A sure sign that a mailing list is administered by machine is that the contact address refers to one of the above programs. Listservers commonly archive correspondence in log files that can be retrieved by E–mail.

Administrative tasks are usually accomplished by single-word commands–commands that vary with the listserver program involved. An E-mail letter to a listserver with the single word **help** in the body of the letter will usually evoke a reply with a list of appropriate commands.

Mailing lists are used by professional groups, on-line newsletters and magazines, and other information and advocacy services.

Discussion Groups

With mailing lists, a single person or central authority produces documents for distribution to subscribers on a fairly regular basis. Discussion groups are more like a giant bull session. Anyone can contribute a message, which is then forwarded to all subscribers.

Any group of people with a common interest can form a discussion group. Groups have been formed to discuss new software programs, research interests, or simply hobbies or political issues. Many listserver discussion groups are associated with academic organizations, associations, and societies. Some discussion groups forward all correspondence; some are moderated by an individual to assure the relevancy of the discussion; some incorporate messages into a periodic newsletter. Some groups are open; some have membership restrictions (via password).

Listerver discussion groups are also referred to as electronic mailing groups, or, just to confuse matters, mailing lists. Alternatively, they are labeled by reference to the computer managing the group: listservers.

Two warnings are in order. First, you must carefully distinguish between the address of the server that administers the distribution of messages (usually in the form *listserv@address*) and the address of the discussion group to which you send contributions (usually in the form *groupname@address*).

Secondly, provocative news items can trigger a deluge of comments from an ever-increasing membership. Since each subscriber receives all correspondence, hundreds of letters may suddenly appear in your mailbox!

Finding Mailing Lists and Discussion Groups The document "Publicly Accessible Mailing Lists" is posted regularly on the Usenet newsgroup *news.answers*. It is also available by anonymous file transfer protocol (*ftp://rtfm.mit.edu/pub/usenet-by-group/news.answers/mail/mailing-lists*). A listing of listserv groups can be obtained by E-mail from *listserv@ubvm.cc.buffalo.edu* with the message:

list global */modifier*

where *modifier* indicates a specific search term within newsgroup titles or descriptions.

A number of World Wide Web programs allow you to search publicly accessible mailing lists (and often newsgroups, as well). Some provide hotlinks for obtaining subscriptions or further information (Figure 2).

Liszt: Searchable Directory of E-mail Discussion Groups

http://www.liszt.com/

Mailing Lists WWW Gateway

http://www.netspace.org/cgi-bin/lwgate

FIGURE 2   Liszt, a World Wide Web search program for accessing discussion groups that utilize the major listserver programs.

You should, of course, run a number of searches with slightly different search terms to assure that you catch all relevant sites.

Newsgroups

Mailing list and discussion group messages are E-mailed to individual subscribers. With newsgroups, E–mail messages are posted on a variety of independent networks for anyone to read and respond. Primary among these networks is Usenet (User's Network), a large portion of which is carried by the Internet.

Usenet newsgroups provide a forum through which people can gossip, debate, and discuss shared interests, a conferencing system by which people from all walks of life can inform, argue with, query, and harangue each other. Newsgroups are often used to distribute the latest versions of FAQs relating to popular software or any other interest area.

Seven categories of newsgroup postings are distributed worldwide: *news, soc, talk, misc, sci, comp,* and *rec.* There is also an *alt* category, a miscellaneous heading for anything that does not fit elsewhere, and *biz* for business-related groups. In addition, there are subcategories that are limited to a specific institution or geographic area, as well as specialized newsgroup feeds such as the news service ClariNet, the BioNet network, and the history mailing list H–Net.

Some such networks combine mailing lists and newsgroups. All messages are both sent to subscribers via E–mail and posted on the appropriate newsgroup.

New users should consult the FAQ posted in *news.announce.newusers* or visit the World Wide Web Usenet Info Center site (*http://sunsite.unc.edu/usenet-i/*).

Using Newsgroups Each newsgroup contains collections of postings or articles that are essentially E-mail messages. Postings on the same topic are assembled into threads.

A special newsreader program is required to read and respond to the postings. Such a reader (the program, that is) typically allows users to subscribe to a specific set of groups from a list of three to four thousand available on any single network. Other newsgroups can still be retrieved, but the system does not have to load all of the messages when starting.

Newsreaders indicate the number of new articles available in each subscribed group. You can save or print a file, search for a particular term, mark files as read, go to the next article in a thread of responses, or respond directly to the author of an article with a new posting (Figure 3).

All newsgroup files are in text mode; graphics and sound files must be decoded prior to viewing.

Finding Newsgroups The search program eXcite (*http://www.excite.com*) can be used to search Usenet groups by keyword or concept. Dejanews (*http://www.dejanews.com/forms/dnquery.html*) searches the text of Usenet archives. The Usenet Info Center, cited above, also offers browsing and searching capabilities for Usenet groups.

Social Considerations Usenet groups are at once the essence and the bane of the Internet. Of all sites on the Internet, newsgroups are the preferred venue for uninhibited surfing and lurking (technical terms for scanning and reading without responding). The level of discussion can vary from the intellectual to the puerile, from mainstream to radical. While some newsgroups are moderated for content, discussion is generally uncensored, encouraging a range of belief and expression with which many are uncomfortable. As the forum for the freest expression on the Internet, newsgroups are often subject to restrictions or outright censorship.

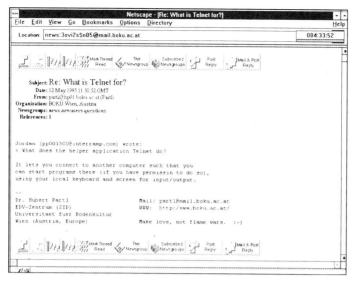

FIGURE 3   A newsgroup posting viewed with the newsreader built into the World Wide Web browser Netscape. Note the command options at the top and bottom of the screen.

Since the anonymity of Internet communication can give rise to relatively antisocial behavior, guides to Internet etiquette ("netiquette") outline traditions of acceptable behavior, such as posting a message to only one newsgroup at a time. Chuq Von Rospach's "A Primer on How to Work with the Usenet Community," a guide to using Usenet politely and efficiently, is available at *news.newusers.questions*. Arlene Rinaldi's "The Net: User Guidelines and Netiquette" is available at *http://rs6000.adm.fau.edu/rinaldi/net/index.htm*.

Talk and Chat Programs

Two other Internet communication programs do not rely on E-mail, but are somewhat simliar in their effect. Talk programs allow two people to "talk" by typing remarks back and forth without exiting their screens. They offer text-based on-line communication.

Chat programs are simply group talk programs. They work somewhat like citizens band radio. Participants can often choose from a list of available chat groups. They can enter or exit a discussion at will, identified only by a handle or nickname they have selected.

Using Talk and Chat Programs Internet talk programs can be initiated at the provider prompt with a **talk** command and an E-mail address. The recipient, assuming he or she is on-line at the time, receives an on-screen message indicating that a session has been initiated. The recipient has only to respond with the same command and the appropriate return E-mail address. A newer program, ntalk ("new talk," of course), is also available.

The Internet version of a chat program, Internet Relay Chat (IRC), requires special software. (For further information, see the newsgroup: *alt.irc*)

New chat programs reflect the general evolution of the Internet toward increasingly sophisticated audio and graphics programs–and with that, a requirement for faster and faster computers, modems, and sound boards. Worlds Chat (*http://www.worlds.net/*) provides a virtual three-dimensional room with photographs of the participants, and Global Chat (*http://www.qdeck.com/chat/globalstage/ servers.html*) adds both sound and graphics to an otherwise text-based chat session.

Add real-time voice and chat programs mimic telephones. Internet Phone (*http://www.vocaltec.com*) enables real-time voice conversations between two people. CUSeeMe (*http://magneto.csc.ncsu.edu/ Multimedia/classes/Spring94/projects/cu-seeme.html*) allows real-time voice and video conferencing utilizing the Internet.

The Internet Services

4

TELNET: THE INTERNET AS REMOTE CONTROL

Here we begin a survey of the programs available on the Internet. We start with the most general, the plain vanilla operation of simply gaining access to another computer. The program for doing this is called telnet.

Telnet

You can extend the cables of your computer via telephone lines to access the files of a remote computer. The keyboard and screen are your own, but you are "using" another computer.

Remote control of another computer is hardly new with the Internet. You run another computer when you dial up a bulletin board or participate on an office network. What is different with the Internet is the number of activities, and the physical range, available to you.

Many library catalogs, community bulletin boards, and academic and governmental information sites are accessible via telnet. Most of the activities of the Internet can be accomplished by telneting to public access sites.

Using Telnet

As with many Internet terms, the word "telnet" has a number of forms. You use the **telnet** command of the telnet program to telnet to a remote computer.

Upon gaining access to the Internet, simply type the command **telnet** and an address:

> prompt% **telnet archie.rutgers.edu**

(Here, as throughout this book, commands and user input are **boldfaced**.) The telnet program contacts the computer at that address using the numerical IP address, waits for a response, and reports its status.

> Connected to dorm.Rutgers.EDU.

What happens then depends on where you've telneted to, and the degree to which that site allows public access. As with most other programs, you can obtain a list of possible commands by issuing the command **help** or **?** at the new prompt.

For more information on Telnet, see "Telnet Tips" at *http://galaxy.einet.net/hytelnet/TELNET.html.*

Hytelnet, a database of telnet–accessible sites with appropriate login commands is available by file transfer protocol (*ftp://access.usask.ca/pub/hytelnet*). Alternatively, you can access telnet sites through a search program on the World Wide Web at *http://galaxy.einet.net/hytelnet/HYTELNET.html* (Figure 4).

FILE TRANSFER PROTOCOL AND ARCHIE: THE INTERNET AS LENDING LIBRARY

File Transfer Protocol (FTP)

FTP is a procedure for downloading files from remote computers.

You cannot access any computer, nor can you access everything on a specific computer. The computer in question must be connected to the network and must grant public access to specific directories and activities.

Computers that archive files and grant public access to selected directories are said to offer anonymous file transfer. Roughly three thousand sites provide anonymous FTP service. Two-thirds of these sites are in the United States, and three-fifths of those are located at educational institutions.

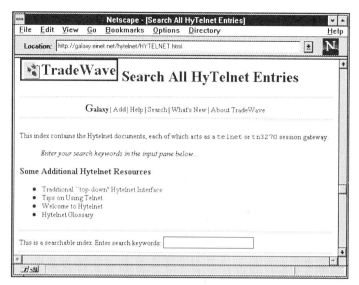

FIGURE 4   A World Wide Web search program for Hytelnet, a
catalog of informational sites publically accessible
by telnet.

Anonymous FTP archives are an excellent source of Internet
software as well as specialized educational and research programs.
Documents, position papers, newsletters, photographs, sound files,
animated movies, and movie clips are all available by FTP.

Using FTP

FTP servers can be accessed via telnet, from a local FTP host, with
graphic-interface programs, or by indicating the URL for an FTP
address with a World Wide Web browser. Finally, most documents
obtainable via anonymous FTP can be obtained via E-mail.
    FTP file retrieval is pursued much as it would be on your own
computer. Whatever software program you employ, the sequence is
the same:

1. Access the remote computer.
2. Login with a username ("anonymous") and password (by tradi-
    tion, your E-mail address).
3. Move from subdirectory to subdirectory with change directory
    (cd) commands to locate the desired file.
4. Read or download the desired file.

5. Repeat steps 3 and 4 as desired.

6. Logoff.

To access an anonymous FTP site with a text-interface program, enter the **ftp** command followed by the address of the desired site at the Internet provider's prompt:

> prompt% **ftp address-of-FTP-archive**

You can access a list of subsequent commands by issuing the command **help** or **?** at the FTP prompt.

With a graphic–interface program or World Wide Web browser, you maneuver through directories by clicking on subdirectory names or icons. You request files by clicking on the filename or icon. Graphic-interface FTP programs usually allow you to maintain a directory of FTP addresses. Simply select an address and the program logs you in and accesses an initial directory (Figure 5).

A complete list of FTP sites generally serves little purpose. We have, after all, little use for a list of all of the libraries in the country; we are more concerned with knowing what books exist and where to find them. Similarly, on the Internet we are more concerned with identifying specific files and their location than with a list of the locations where files might be stored. Neverethless, a list of Internet sites accepting anonymous FTP is maintained by Perry Rovers at *http://www.info.net/Public/ftp-list.html.*

Instruction in the use of FTP is available in the form of a FAQ document via E-mail from *mail-server@rtfm.mit.edu.* Include no subject and only the message:

> **send usenet/news.answers/ftp-list/faq**

with no final punctuation. You can access FYI 24, How to Use Anonymous FTP (*http://www.ftp.com/techsup/fyi/fyi24.html*).

Finally, file transfer from remote computers is not a right. It is a privilege that carries with it distinct responsibilities, such as not downloading files during peak hours. For additional guidance, see the FTP guides above or "The Net: User Guidelines and Netiquette" referred to in the section on newsgroups (page 17).

Archie: The Card Catalog

File transfer protocol provides access to files on computers around the world. But how do you know where to look for a particular file, or for any file of a particular type? You can burrow through the sub-

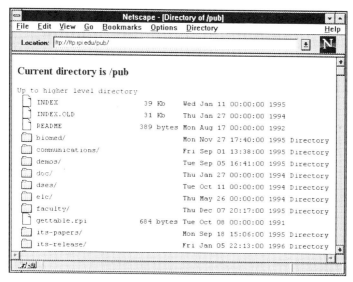

FIGURE 5 A directory listing from an FTP session using the Netscape World Wide Web browser. The options on this screen include returning to the previous level of the directory, displaying text files (indicated by page icons), or proceeding to lower level directories (indicated by file folder icons). The INDEX and README files are generally a useful starting point for any search.

directories and read the indexes on one computer after another, but this is obviously both time consuming and inefficient.

As with other aspects of the Internet, much of your information will come from word of mouth. A magazine article will mention a file. A *read.me* file will refer to another document or program. A newsgroup posting will announce a new program or document. In each case, the address of a relevant FTP server will usually be supplied.

As useful as these resources may be, they will not always suffice. Some means of searching available files is still necessary.

Since the Internet has no center, no central card catalog is possible. A reasonable facsimile, however, is recreated every month at a number of locations by a service and search program called Archie. Sites that offer anonymous FTP register with an Archie service. Over a period of a month, the Archie service scans those sites and generates a list of files and directory names. The resulting database is then mirrored on several other Archie servers, all of which then contain the same information.

Using Archie

Public-access Archie servers are reached by the **telnet** command and a suitable address. Obtain a list of such sites from *telnet://archie.ans.net*. Login as "archie" (all lowercase) and type "servers" at the first prompt.

Alternatively, if Archie is installed on your host system, accesss Archie by issuing the **archie** command with no address specified.

Upon reaching an archie server, sign on with the username "archie". No password is necessary. To search for a specific program, type the command **prog** followed by the name of the program. The command **help** or **?** at the archie prompt will list other available commands.

Archie servers often indicate your place in line (queue position) and the expected time of completion of a search. While there are thousands of FTP servers, there are a limited number of Archie servers. A queue position of 35 is not uncommon. If the anticipated delay is long, simply try another server. In most cases, a server will offer a list of other active servers.

As with graphic-interface FTP programs, graphic-interface Archie programs store lists of server addresses and automatically submit the userid "archie" at the login prompt.

Archie searches combined with FTP retrieval are available at various Web sites, including the Archie Request Form at NCSA (*http://hoohoo.ncsa.uiuc.edu/archie.html*) (Figure 6).

GOPHER AND VERONICA: THE INTERNET AS RESEARCH LIBRARY

Gopher

Gopher is a tool for burrowing or tunneling through file resources on the Internet. It is akin to browsing from a document in one library to another document in another library.

Gopher is based on menus. Gopher menus point to other menus, which ultimately point to specific documents, whether text, picture, animation, sound file, or search program on the same or other computers.

While all types of files can be accessed using Gopher, a Gopher screen displays either a menu or a document–no graphics, fancy fonts, or icons. Sound and graphics files must be downloaded for viewing later.

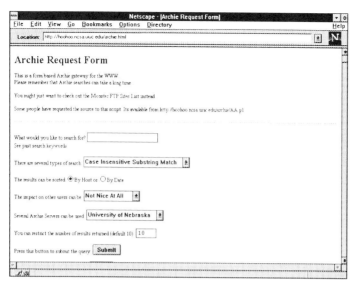

FIGURE 6 A World Wide Web Archie program. Note the search options.

As with other services, you can access only what someone lets you. Gopher sites are for the most part located at academic institutions and government agencies. The resulting materials are therefore of an academic/research/statistical nature. Entertainment, commercial, and lifestyle resources tend to be cataloged on the more recent World Wide Web.

Using Gopher

You can access Gopher menus in various ways.

If your Internet provider offers no Gopher service, you can use the **telnet** command to access any of a dozen or so public-access Gopher sites.

If Gopher service is offered by your Internet provider, the **gopher** command alone accesses the provider's initial menu and the **gopher** command followed by an address reaches a specific Gopher site anywhere in the world.

Finally, you can access specific Gopher sites with specialized graphic-interface programs or a World Wide Web browser.

Since all Gophers provide access to all Gopherspace, you can get to any Gopher from any other.

One of the standard starting points on most systems is a topic-oriented menu called Gopher Jewels. With text–interface, the initial menu looks like this:

Gopher Jewels

1. GOPHER JEWELS Information and Help/
2. Community, Global and Environmental/
3. Education, Social Sciences, Arts & Humanities/
4. Economics, Business and Store Fronts/
5. Engineering and Industrial Applications/
6. Government/
7. Health, Medical, and Disability/
8. Internet and Computer Related Resources/
9. Law/
10. Library, Reference, and News/
11. Miscellaneous Items/
12. Natural Sciences including Mathematics/
13. Personal Development and Recreation/
14. Research, Technology Transfer and Grants Opportunities/
15. Search Gopher Jewels Menus by Key Word(s) <?>

Page: 1/1

Markings at the end of each line indicate the nature of each menu item. A right slash, / , indicates that the item leads to a lower-level menu. The question mark within brackets, < ? > , indicates a searchable database.

Since Gopher is menu-based, text–interface and graphic-interface sessions look pretty much the same (Figure 7).

Negotiating from one Gopher menu to another is accomplished with cursor keys or by clicking on icons. To select a menu item, simply move the cursor to the item and hit the enter key or point and click with a mouse. The Gopher program issues a telnet, FTP, or other command to access that item.

If you reach a dead end, double back to an earlier choice by clicking on an icon representing the earlier menu or, with a text-based system, by hitting the left cursor.

Gopher programs allow you to create a personal menu of your favorite Gopher sites (bookmarks) for later use. The Gopher FAQ is located at *gopher://mudhoney.micro.umn.edu/70/00/gopher.faq.*

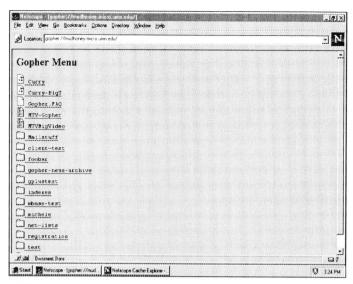

FIGURE 7   Gopher menu viewed with a World Wide Web browser.

In the end, Gopher is essentially a browsing tool. You can pursue material on specific topics, but since you have to hunt around, it is not really a search program. Gopher is also a retrieval program. (You will recall that file transfer protocol was a retrieval program, not really a search tool, and Archie a search tool but not a tool for retrieval.)

The value of Gopher is in great part not only what you find at the end of your travels but what you discover along the way. The investigation itself will often suggest additional topics and resources you may never have imagined.

Veronica: Searching with Gopher

As a browser, Gopher offers a slow and haphazard approach to research. A more direct route is available, however.

Veronica (Very Easy Rodent-Oriented Net-Wide Index to Computerized Archives) builds a searchable index of Gopher menus in much the same way that Archie builds an index of FTP files. Every week, about a dozen Veronica sites search and index the titles in menus of registered Gopher servers. The result is a searchable database of virtually all of the Gopher servers in the world.

Veronica goes one step further. Archie told you where files were; you had to get them yourself using FTP. The output from a Veronica search is a custom Gopher menu. Veronica is thus both a search and a retrieval tool.

Since Veronica is a tool of Gophers, it appears as an option on the initial menu of most Gopher servers. There is no need for a **veronica** command. If one of the Veronica indexes is unavailable due to high traffic, simply try another (Figure 8). The home base for Veronica is at *gopher://veronica.scs.unr.edu/11/veronica.*

Jughead (Jonzy's Universal Gopher Hierarchy Excavation and Display), a variant of Veronica, searches file names and directories on a select number of Gophers or the immediate Gopher server.

Using Veronica

Veronica searches menus, not the contents of the Gopher servers themselves. Veronica indexes do, however, include additional items, such as titles from World Wide Web servers, Usenet archives, and telnet information services that are referenced on Gopher menus.

Veronica searches are not case-sensitive (searching for Tuba will locate TUBA, tuba, and Tuba), and Veronica understands the Boolean logical operators AND, NOT, OR (a blank is assumed to be AND). Additional commands allow you to restrict the search to certain types of files or a maximum number of responses. Veronica also supports partial word searches in which an asterisk "*" represents a wild card character or characters. "Go*" will return all items that have a word beginning with "go" in the title.

Veronica search terms will appear in every menu item. This is as it should be; after all, searches are defined as searches for specific words in menu titles. But such a search will obviously fail to include closely associated items or similar items described in different terms.

Here, as in all research, there is a distinct art to selecting the proper search terms. Try alternate searches using synonyms or more general terms to assure yourself that you are capturing all of the relevant references. If a search yields an inordinate number of responses, search again with a more limited search term. If you desire more options, search again with an alternative phrase or more general terms, or browse some of the sites indicated and see what you find.

When you know exactly what term or phrase best describes what you are looking for, a Veronica search can be more direct–and potentially more fruitful–than simply following Gopher menus.

For an extended discussion of Veronica search techniques, see the FAQ document "how-to-query-veronica" offered with Veronica menus.

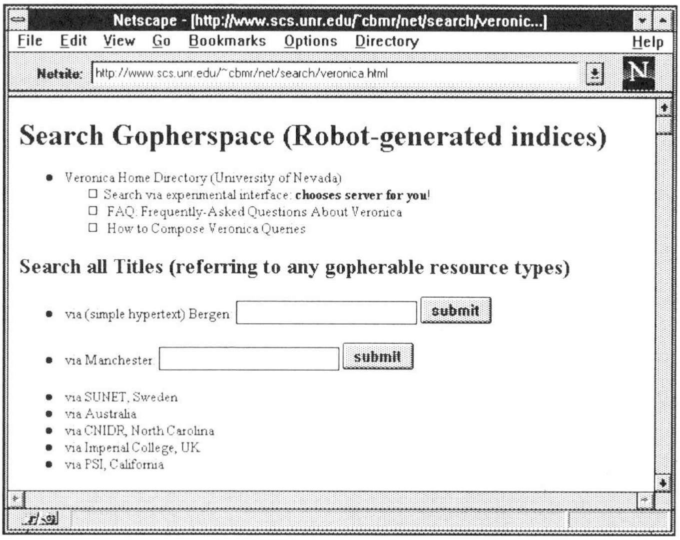

```
┌──────────────────────────────────────────────────────────┐
│        Netscape - [http://www.scs.unr.edu/~cbmr/net/search/veronic...]  ▼ ▲│
│ File  Edit  View  Go  Bookmarks  Options  Directory            Help │
│ ┌────────────────────────────────────────────────────────┐ │
│ Netsite:│http://www.scs.unr.edu/~cbmr/net/search/veronica.html    │±│ N │
│ ├────────────────────────────────────────────────────────┤ │
│                                                              │
│  Search Gopherspace (Robot-generated indices)              │
│                                                              │
│    • Veronica Home Directory (University of Nevada)         │
│        □ Search via experimental interface: chooses server for you! │
│        □ FAQ Frequently-Asked Questions About Veronica     │
│        □ How to Compose Veronica Queries                   │
│                                                              │
│  Search all Titles (referring to any gopherable resource types) │
│                                                              │
│    • via (simple hypertext) Bergen [          ] [submit]   │
│                                                              │
│    • via Manchester [          ] [submit]                  │
│                                                              │
│    • via SUNET, Sweden                                     │
│    • via Australia                                         │
│    • via CNIDR, North Carolina                             │
│    • via Imperial College, UK                              │
│    • via PSI, California                                   │
│                                                              │
└──────────────────────────────────────────────────────────┘
```

FIGURE 8   A World Wide Web Veronica interface.

WAIS: SEARCHING DOCUMENTS

WAIS

Archie searches file names in directories of anonymous FTP servers; Veronica searches key words in Gopher menus. Neither examines documents themselves, only their listing in a directory or menu. WAIS (pronounced "waze"), on the other hand, is specifically document oriented.

The WAIS (Wide Area Information Servers) information retrieval system on the Internet is an application of a more general search protocol. WAIS examines the full text of all of the documents on a particular database. It searches for key words and ranks documents according to the number and placement of the "hits." Like Veronica, WAIS offers a menu from which you can then retrieve documents.

In actual fact, WAIS searches not documents but *indexes* of the text of documents. As a result, the WAIS database can include anything that can be indexed with words. Descriptions of insects or works of art can be indexed to pictures of the items. Descriptions of songs can be indexed to sound files. In the end, however, you can only access what has been indexed.

There are roughly six hundred free public databases, each devoted to a particular collection of materials, each with the *.src* extension indicating a WAIS database.

WAIS databases exist for newsgroups, professional journals, and bibliographies. They include databases of Hubble Space Telescope Instrument Status Reports, U.S. Department of Agriculture commodity market reports, and the Columbia Law School card catalogue. Fewer WAIS databases exist for nonacademic areas or for topics for which the relevant materials are widely dispersed.

Using WAIS

WAIS can be accessed by the telnet command at *quake.think.com* (login as "wais") or at a number of other public-access sites, as an option on some Gopher menus, or via the World Wide Web (*http://www.ai.mit.edu/the-net/wais.html*) (Figure 9). It can also be accessed by E-mail at *WAISmail@quake.think.com*. (Here again, the message "help" will elicit a list of the proper commands.)

A WAIS search involves a number of steps:

1. Select the appropriate database(s) (sources)
2. Select key-word search term(s) (questions)
3. Indicate the maximum number of responses desired
4. Search the specific database(s)
5. Review the results and access specific files

If you do not know which database to search, you can first search a directory of servers, *directory-of-servers.scr*, and then select appropriate databases from the initial output (Figure 10).

A listing of public-access WAIS databases is available in compressed form at *ftp://quake.think.com/pub/directory-of-servers/wais-sources.tar*. The WAIS FAQ is available from *ftp://quake.think.com/pub/wais-doc/waisfaq.txt*.

As with Veronica searches, WAIS searches must be executed with care. A single word can have different meanings in different contexts. You must, then, decide how relevant the resulting hits actually are, and re-search if necessary.

A search on the word "table," for instance, would locate references to furniture (kitchen table), economic charts (statistical tables), and parliamentary procedure (table a motion). To be more specific in your search, you might search on additional terms that are likely to occur in the same context. Alternatively, newer WAIS programs allow for relevance checking, a means of refining a second search based on the results of the first. Newer programs also allow the use of Boolean logic in search terms.

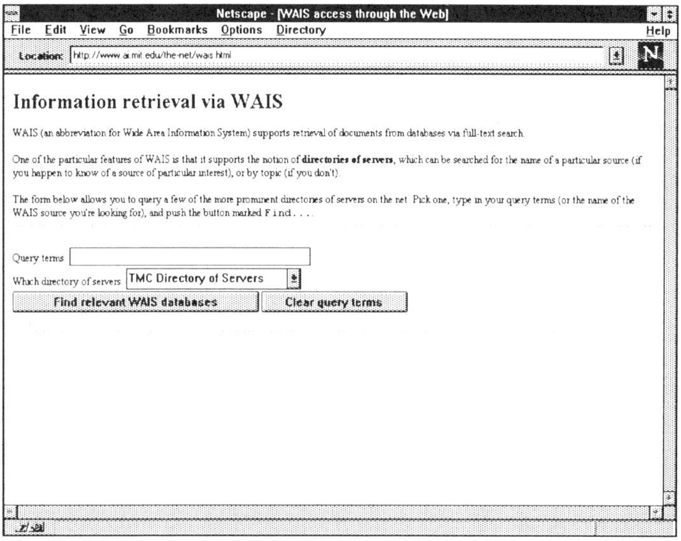

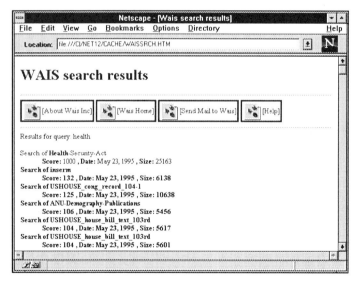

FIGURE 9   A World Wide Web site offering access to WAIS searches.

FIGURE 10   Initial WAIS search results searching on the question "health" in the *directory–of–servers.src* database, listed by score.

Above all, you must be careful not to assume that a lack of citations necessarily implies a lack of evidence. It may be that you just didn't look as imaginatively as you might have.

WAIS is most suitable when you are looking for unspecified information related to a very specific term or are searching a select database for known information. If you want to find out about the American welfare system, Gopher or the World Wide Web would be a more appropriate resource.

THE WORLD WIDE WEB: THE INTERNET AS MULTIMEDIA

Of all the aspects of the Internet, the World Wide Web (WWW) has evoked the greatest hyperbole. Laurie Flynn, in *The New York Times,* referred to it as "an electronic amalgam of the public library, the suburban shopping mall and the Congressional Record," while Peter H. Lewis, in the same newspaper, referred to it as "a time-sucking black hole...a speedtrap on the data highway, a Bermuda Triangle in the information ocean, the junk food aisle in cyberspace's digital supermarket."

The Web, as it is often called, is the fastest growing service on the Internet. In just a few years, it has become an integral, and for some indispensable, part of the culture.

As with Gopher, the World Wide Web is a means of accessing files on computers connected via the Internet. The World Wide Web is not a physical place, nor a set of files, nor even a network of computers. The heart of the World Wide Web lies in the protocols that define its use. Yet it is the appearance of the Web that is most striking.

The Look!

Each Web site opens with a home page, "a combination frontispiece, greeting room, table of contents, hub, and launching pad," in the words of Michael Neubarth, editor-in-chief of *Internet World.*

Gopher menus can lead to files that contain pictures or sound or even movie clips, but the overall presentation of the menus is text. A typical Gopher menu, even viewed with a graphics program, still looks like a menu of items (Figure 7). The World Wide Web, on the other hand, is the only truly multimedia presentation on the Internet. You have only to look at a World Wide Web screen to see the difference (Figure 11)!

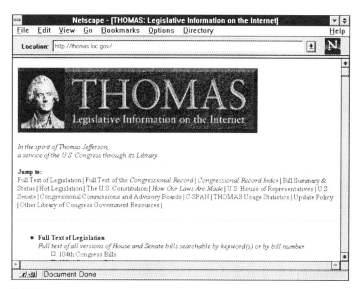

FIGURE 11 Thomas World Wide Web home page utilizing graphics.

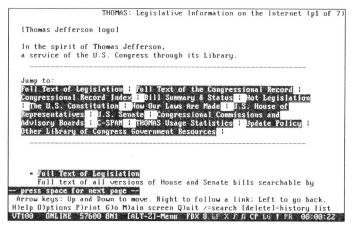

FIGURE 12 Thomas World Wide Web page viewed with the text-interface browser Lynx. Note the indication of the number of screens for the complete page at the top.

A Web page has all of the aspects of sophisticated desktop publishing: diverse typefaces, charts and forms, icons and integrated graphics. Sound and movies can even be integrated into the presentation. Recent increases in computer speed have spawned applications utilizing real-time sound and 3-D or virtual reality graphics.

To be sure, the World Wide Web can be accessed with a text interface, but it has none of the panache of the graphics version. Elements that appear highlighted by color in a graphic interface appear as underlined or shadowed text (Figure 12).

What's Behind It All: Hypertext

The World Wide Web is based on the notion of links within hypertext pages.

In hypertext, key concepts and ideas are linked to the address of related material, in much the same manner that each item in a Gopher menu is encoded with the location of the requisite menu or file. Links within the discussion are indicated by highlighted terms, icons, or simply locations on the page called hotspots. Click on a hotspot, and you access the linked item, be it another Web page or any one of a number of the other Internet services. Footnote numbers can provide direct access to the original sources. Links can be inserted into maps and drawings. You can click on a room in a blueprint and see a photograph of that room.

The overall effect is not unlike reading an encyclopedia with the ability to snap your fingers to instantly shift to another page, another book, or even a phonograph or slide projector! You do not need to follow a predetermined sequence of ideas. You can branch off as your interests dictate.

Hypertext Transfer Protocol (HTTP)

Hypertext linkage is accomplished with Hypertext Transfer Protocol (HTTP), the main operating system of the World Wide Web–hence the URL notation *http://*. This protocol contains the instructions to connect to a remote computer, request a specified document, receive the document, and sever the connection.

Hypertext Markup Language (HTML)

The coding of a World Wide Web page is done with Hypertext Markup Language (HTML). Just as a word processor inserts codes to indicate fonts and font sizes, paragraph breaks and boldface, so HTML inserts tags or elements to accomplish the same effects. The resulting format is seen only when the page is read by a Web browser.

The following is the HTML document underlying the Thomas home page. Addresses are indicated in universal resource locator

(URL) notation. On-screen text has been marked in boldface to distinguish it from the hypertext markup language coding. Hyperlinks, indicated on screen by a contrasting color, are indicated here in italics.

<!doctype html public "-//W30//DTD WWW HTML 2.0//EN">
<HTML>
<HEAD>
<TITLE>**THOMAS: Legislative Information on the Internet**</TITLE>
<!BASE HREF="http://thomas.loc.gov/home/thomas.html">
</HEAD>
<BODY>
<img src= "http://thomas.loc.gov/home/thom_mas.gif"
alt="[Thomas
Jefferson logo] ">
<P><EM>**In the spirit of Thomas Jefferson,**
a service of the
U.S. Congress through its Library.</EM>
<HR>
<STRONG>**Jump to:**</STRONG>
<A HREF="#legislation">*Full Text of Legislation*</A> |
<A HREF="#record">*Full Text of the*<I>*Congressional Record*</I></A> |
<A HREF="#index"><I>*Congressional Record Index*</I></A> |
<A HREF="#bss">*Bill Summary & Status*</A> |
<A HREF="#hot">*Hot Legislation*</A> |
<A HREF="http://lcweb2.loc.gov:8080/constquery.html">*The U.S. Constitution*</A> |
<A HREF="http://thomas.loc.gov/home/lawsmade.toc.html">
<I>*How Our Laws Are Made*</I></A> |
<A HREF="#house">*U.S. House of Representatives*</A> |
<A HREF="#senate">*U.S. Senate*</A> |
<A HREF="#congcom">*Congressional Commissions and Advisory Boards*</A> |
<A HREF="#cspan">*C-SPAN*</A> |
<A HREF = "http://thomas.loc.gov/stats/stats.html">*THOMAS Usage Statistics*</A> |
<A HREF="#update">*Update Policy*</A> |
<A HREF="#resources">*Other Library of Congress Government Resources*</A> |</P> <HR>
<UL>
<P>
<LI><A NAME="legislation"><STRONG>**Full Text of Legislation**</STRONG></A>

<EM>**Full text of all versions of House and Senate bills searchable by keyword(s) or by bill number.**</EM>
<UL>
<LI><a href="http://thomas.loc.gov/home/c104query.html">***104th Congress Bills***</a>

....

Notice that an HTML document, unlike a document produced with a word processor, is in plain ASCII text. The result is a universally accessible page that can be read by browsers using any operating system, whether Windows, Macintosh, or UNIX.

For discussion of Hypertext Markup Language, see A Beginner's Guide to HTML (*http://www.msg.net/tutorial/html–primer.html*), HTML Help (*http://www.obscure.org/~jaws/htmlhelp.html*), or The Almost Complete HTML Reference (*http://www.digital-planet.com/htmlref*).

Web Browsers

The World Wide Web is accessed with programs called browsers. The browser Mosaic is to a great extent responsible for the initial explosion of the World Wide Web; Netscape has since become the standard for most users, and is responsible for the continuing expansion.

A Web browser is in reality an HTML reader. A browser reads the HTML code indicating such attributes as bold <STRONG>, a list of items <LI>, or links <A HREF=>. Not all browsers can decode newer codes, such as those for background colors or user–input forms; and users can control some attributes, such as the size and font of the type. Thus, while all browsers can read any HTML page, any single page can look different on different browsers.

Web browsers open on a default home page. It may be the home page of your provider, the home page of the browser program, or any page that you have designated. Utilizing Hypertext Transfer Protocol, Web browsers access Web locations, follow hypertext links, and create an ongoing history of the sites visited in your travels.

Using the World Wide Web

Text-based browsers such as Lynx can be launched from public-access sites using the **telnet** command or as selections on the higher-level menus of many Gophers. Alternatively, access with

Lynx is available directly from a provider prompt. Simply type **lynx** followed by a Web address expressed in URL format:

prompt% **lynx http://thomas.loc.gov**

The command **lynx**, alone, accesses the default home page of your Internet provider.

Graphic-interface programs such as Mosaic or Netscape follow essentially the same process. Simply enter an appropriate address (or use the default site) and click on highlighted terms or icons to move from site to site. No fancy commands are necessary.

If you have used that browser before, you will have saved a list of bookmarks or hotlinks leading to your favorite sites. Alternatively, you can start from one of a number of menus, indexes, or key-word search programs.

The World Wide Web FAQ, offering discussion on both World Wide Web resources and browsers, is located at *http://www.boutell.com/faq/www_faq.html.*

The Glory and the Hype

The attention given the World Wide Web is in huge part deserved– but only in part.

Due to the added space required by fancy fonts and graphics, the text of most hypertext displays on the World Wide Web is decidedly cursory. The full opportunity for lengthy discussion is rarely taken. You find, instead, essentially an illustrated and annotated menu. Whereas a Gopher menu might offer 15 possible paths on a single screen, the opening screen of a Web site often has no more than 5 links, if that many. While many Gopher menus are complete on a single screen, a full view of most Web pages requires scanning a number of screens. These problems are clearly due in part to a lack of sophistication in writing Web pages, but the problems remain.

Content is also an issue. Many corporate home pages offer the electronic equivalent of junk mail, filled with what Bart Zeigler of the *Wall Street Journal* has descibed as "turgid company profiles, hokey product pitches and bland marketing material...that wouldn't make it from the mailbox to the kitchen counter of most homes if they arrived via the Postal Service."

Speed is another consideration. You pay for graphics with reduced speed. The text version of the opening page of the Thomas Congressional site uses 7,838 bytes of information. The opening graphic alone is another 31,280 bytes. In short, the screen with full graphics takes at least five times as long to receive. With a 14,400-baud modem, the

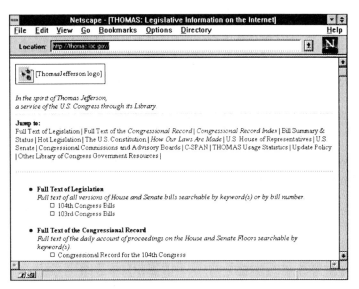

FIGURE 13 Thomas World Wide Web home page without graphics.

wait is annoying and at times seems interminable. The delay with animation, sound messages, or movies is even more profound. In response to this problem, new browsers load the text first, painting in pictures later, or allow you to view the screen in a text format with pictures replaced by icons (Figure 13).

Finally, anyone on the Internet can establish a home page presence on the Web. There is no committee to go through, no certification to acquire, no large investment in hardware required. Many Internet providers and on-line services now offer this opportunity to their subscribers.

The ease with which Web sites can be established has both advantages and disadvantages. On the one hand, it guarantees openness and diversity. On the other hand, the Web is subject to an overabundance of choices, many of questionable value. With broader access to the Web via on-line services, the increase in new sites has been accelerated by businesses anticipating methods for secure credit card transactions on the Internet.

Even with all the problems, in many instances the resources of the Web are without equal. For maps, product pictures, photographs, artwork, and other illustrative material, there is no substitute.

Constructing Your Own Home Page

Anyone can create a home page to use as an opening page with their browser. No programming experience is required. For help making a home page you can read How to Make a Great Home Page (*http://www.valleynet.net/~kiradive/home.html*), or complete the forms at the Home Page Generator (*http://www.cs.uoregon.edu/ ~jolson/generator/*.

Writing home pages is relatively simple. Getting a home page on the Internet is another matter. The easiest approach is to find a server that will carry your home page–either at your university or through your Internet service provider.

Research on the Internet

5

GENERAL CONCERNS

What am I looking for, and where can I find it? Research is

- initiated by questions,
- guided by knowledge and reflection, and
- driven by feedback.

All of which is to say that much of research is a matter of trial and error. But it is a methodical and informed trial and error.

Research Is Initiated by Questions

Research begins with questions, with wanting to know something. You may seek specific information about a specific topic (What is the atomic weight of uranium?) or a wide range of ideas on a broad topic (How might welfare be revised?). One way or another, you want to know something you don't already know.

If you think you know it all, there is no need for research. If you want to see if you're right, that is in itself a question and a legitimate basis for research.

Finally, research assumes that the information you want to know exists, and that it is available where you can find it. The real question, then, is where to look. Or even more to the point, how to find out where to look. Which brings us to the second point.

Research Is Guided by Knowledge and Reflection

The more you know about what you want to find, the easier it is to find it. This may seem obvious, but it is also profound. Without prior reflection, you can waste hours chasing inappropriate sources, hours that could be saved with a little thought before you started.

In what context does a term appear? Surely that will provide a start. Alternatively, you might ask: Who cares? Who would want to know? If you know who cares about a topic or issue, you are well along the way to finding out who might collect information, store it, and have it available.

Here, as elsewhere, research requires that you generalize, that you recognize the *kind* of thing you are dealing with, that you classify or categorize ideas.

Different kinds of information will, obviously, be found in different places. Without knowing *something* about what you are looking for, you cannot even start! Once you recognize the kind of information you are seeking, you are well on your way to realizing where it might be found.

Research Is Driven by Feedback

Research is a matter of discovery, discrimination, and elimination. Everything you find, or do not find, shapes your further inquiry.

If you find what you want, well and good. If you don't, the trick is to turn momentary failure into a productive learning experience.

The discovery of the *absence* of data is often as important as discovery of relevant data itself. You must determine if nothing is there or whether you just didn't find it. If not here, then where? Try alternate search strategies to assure that information is truly unavailable.

As you search, you will discover new interests or topics. As you eliminate one source, you will be led to others.

Internet Concerns

The resources of the Internet are indeed enormous and ever expanding. Resources unheard of only a few years ago are now commonplace. But, as we suggested, you must first have some idea of what's out there, and know how to find what you want when you want it.

Know Your Options

Knowing *where* to look depends greatly on knowing where you *might* look. You should be aware of the existence of, and uses of, a number of electronic resources–both in general and in your field of interest, such as:

> databases (both public and commercial)
>
> abstract services
>
> specialized on-line library collections
>
> professional associations
>
> state and government agencies
>
> nonprofit organizations
>
> usenet newsgroups and listerver discussion groups
>
> anonymous FTP software archives

Know How to Get What You Want

Knowing what is on the Internet, and where it is, is only half the story. You also have to know how to get where you want to go. You must understand the variety of services and the programs necessary to access those services.

To use the services effectively, you should understand how each service organizes and accesses information. That means such things as knowing the addresses of gopher subject menus and why you might choose to use Veronica instead of a World Wide Web search program. It means knowing whether a particular search program accepts Boolean logic in its search terms and how to properly formulate such searches.

To use the Internet–and your own time–effectively, you must distinguish between active discovery and idle diversion, between productive research and sheer busywork.

Authorship, Authenticity, Authoritativeness, and Value

When you pick up a book or newspaper, you have a certain confidence in the authenticity of the material. Examining a book or professional journal in a library, you are aware that it has been selected from among competing texts and reviewed by an editor prior to publication, and selected from among competing publications by a librarian for inclusion in the collection. The title and copyright page attest to the true author and place and date of publication. And you are reasonably certain the document exists in the form intended by the author.

With the Internet, all of these assumptions may fall under suspicion. When it is easy to create personnae, it is hard to verify credentials. Internet citations have no page numbers or publication dates, and a reader pursuing a citation may find the text has been moved or altered–with no way to know the difference.

On the whole, Internet data is no more authoritative than any other–and in many cases less so. While we may delight in the fact that we can post anything we want on sections of the Internet, when we are looking for information we would like to be able to distinguish beforehand between a professor's treatise and Jonny's seventh grade school report. "Anyone who has attempted to obtain information from the internet," an editorial in the *Journal of Chemical Education* observed, "knows that you are as likely to find garbage as you are to find quality information." The affiliation of a server may suggest a certain degree of reliability, but that in itself should indicate neither approval nor review by anyone else at that institution.

While the Internet may have the richness and range of a world-class encyclopedia, that does not mean you want to, or need to, read every article. Much of the current material on the Internet is outdated or only offers snippets of information. Much of the discussion on newsgroups is simply chatter. Just because you can download thousands of files does not mean you need any of them.

One the bright side, since it is easier to publish material on the Internet than it is to publish books, information available on the Internet is often more up-to-date than information in printed texts. But that is useful only for information that changes frequently, or has changed recently.

INTERNET TACTICS AND STRATEGIES

Is the Internet the Best Tool to Use?

You may turn to the Internet to save time, to save effort, or to find better sources of information. But just because you have access to the Internet does not mean the Internet is necessarily the best tool for a particular project. Many times, other procedures are quicker, easier, and more certain to yield results.

Try the Obvious First

The general rule should be: Try the obvious first. This seems self evident, but it often needs restating. To find the Latin name for lions you can turn on your computer, logon to your Internet service, access a search program, input a search term, wait for a response, evaluate the sources provided, and continue on to a specific location. Or you can flip open a collegiate dictionary and look it up. There's a lesson there.

Networking for Knowledge

The car manufacturer Packard long ago had a slogan: Ask the man who owns one. With research: Ask someone who knows. You can use E-mail to communicate with others, or check archives of frequently asked questions of a relevant newsgroup. You can participate in the communication of a discussion group.

Overall, however, you are more likely to gain fresh insights and understanding through the interchange of talking to someone else than you are punching keys on a keyboard and staring at a computer screen.

What You Can, and Cannot, Find

The Internet was developed for scientists to exchange data and ideas. While much of the emphasis has shifted to commercial and entertainment applications, the Internet remains a vital link in academic and scientific communication.

In recent years governmental agencies at all levels have made increasing amounts of information available on the Internet. Many professional associations and interest groups maintain home pages on the World Wide Web.

Still, no one gives anything of value away for free. While you can access some encyclopedias on the Internet, the premiere volume, *Encyclopedia Britannica*, is available only by commercial subscription.

Full texts of professional journals are, for the most part, available only in hard copy. Nevertheless, journals increasingly offer tables of contents, archives of abstracts, and supplemental tables, illustrations, or data, as well as searchable indexes of past issues on the Internet.

Commercial full-text databases such as Nexis/Lexis and Dialog can often be accessed via the Internet for a fee. Students and faculty, however, often have access to such proprietary databases on-line or on CD-ROM in college libraries.

Selecting an Appropriate Service

Each service of the Internet accesses different resources. Each is, therefore, useful for different purposes. Which you turn to will depend on what you are looking for.

E-mail

If you wish to contact **specific people,** or **post a message to a discussion group or newsgroup,** E-mail is the program to use.

Listserv / Discussion Groups

If wish to locate **individuals as representatives of an organization or sharing a specific interest,** listserv discussion groups may be appropriate.

Newsgroups

If you seek **current discussion of a particular topic or issue,** or **to identify individuals with a specific interest,** newsgroups are the desired choice.

FTP/Archie

If you seek **specific computer files,** especially programs related to the Internet, file transfer protocol would be the obvious starting point. If you are not sure where to find specific files, the associated search program, Archie, is a useful tool.

Gopher/Veronica

If you wish to locate **documents, files, information, or data from or about a specific education, governmental or non-profit organization or association,** you might check to see if they (or anyone else) have a Gopher server with the desired resources. The search program Veronica can be of service here, as well as for just about any academic, governmental, or computer-related topic.

WAIS

If you are seeking **specific documents** or the content of a certain type of document or database, WAIS, the sole program aimed at full-text searches would be in order.

World Wide Web

If you wish to locate **documents, files, information, or data from or about a specific business or commercial enterprise,** the World Wide Web would be the most direct source. The same is true for **product information and technical**

assistance. And the Web is the choice for most **multimedia presentations,** whether sound, movies, or simply graphics, as well as for the **site of home pages for popular issues and concerns.**

Finally, remember that many World Wide Web search programs include references to other aspects of the Internet, and often even provide direct links to them.

Budgeting Your Time and On-line Time

The general rule for efficient use of the Internet is simple: logon, get what you want, and logoff.

You want to know what you're looking for beforehand and have a plan for accessing it. You want to get the information you seek, and get out. This is especially true when you are incurring hourly expenses imposed by on-line services and Internet providers.

You can save time and money by downloading information for later perusal. Off-line time is cheaper than on-line time, and hard copies are easier to read than text on screens.

Both text and graphic-interface programs offer some means of automatically capturing on-screen text during a session. You can save hypertext pages on the World Wide Web in a cache directory for closer examination off-line.

Spend your time on-line evaluating information, not looking up addresses. If your software program allows it, maintain directories of sites for FTP, Gopher, and WAIS programs. If this is not possible, keep a log of addresses handy. When using Gopher and World Wide Web programs, make bookmarks for sites you return to often.

Citations and Plagiarism

You can save time and effort by downloading documents instead of finding published texts and photocopying them. You can then insert that text directly into your own writing.

While a great convenience, this process has obvious dangers. You can confuse your text with text that you have downloaded, and in so doing commit the crime of plagiarism. And you can lose track of information for proper citations.

To avoid plagiarism, store downloaded text with a special font– such as *italic* or SMALL CAPITAL LETTERS–and change the font only when the material has been properly cited within your discussion.

The address of Internet documents is often equivalent to the publication data associated with books. While no standards have

been universally accepted, tentative standards are discussed at
http://www.cas.usf.edu/english/walker/mla.html.

INTERNET RESEARCH RESOURCES

As with all research, research on the Internet has to start somewhere.
Once you know what you are looking for, you have to select tools to
work with.

Browsing versus Searching

There are essentially two approaches to research on the Internet:
browsing and searching.

Gopher and the World Wide Web menus offer choices for browsing. Archie, Veronica, WAIS, and various World Wide Web search
programs offer key-word search opportunities that, in the latter two
cases, then offer initial menus for browsing.

Searching begins with selecting a search program or engine and
a search term or terms. Browsing requires, once again, a choice of
where to start browsing.

Desk Reference Tools

We might start with menus that offer, in effect, electronic versions
of standard library resources such as the U.S. Geographic Names
Database, U.S. Telephone Area Codes, Webster's Dictionary, the CIA
World Fact Book, or headlines from the Associated Press/Reuters
News Wire Service.

Many universities offer menus of basic desk reference tools on
Gopher or the World Wide Web. See Reference Resources via the
World Wide Web (*http://vm.cfsan.fda.gov/referenc.html*) or access
desk reference tools at:

The Virtual Reference Desk at Purdue University
http://thorplus.lib.purdue.edu/reference/index.html

Indiana State
gopher://odin.indstate.edu:70/11/ref.dir/info.dir

National Institute of Health
gopher://odie.niaid.nih.gov:70/11/deskref

Desk reference menus can offer a useful starting point for browsing.

Comprehensive Subject Guides

Comprehensive subject guides, such as the following, are excellent candidates as bookmarks for your browser program.

Gopher Jewels

http://galaxy.einet.net/GJ/index.html

Special Internet Connections, by Scott Yanoff

http://www.uwm.edu/Mirror/inet.services.html

An extensive list of specific sites under academic and general headings

YAHOO (Yet Another Hierarchically Odiferous Oracle)

http://www.yahoo.com

A convenient and extensive subject-area listing of World Wide Web sites, plus a search tool

Government Information Locator Service (GILS)

http://info.er.usgs.gov/gils/index.html

The best resource list, of course, is the one *you* develop from your own experience to meet your own needs.

Discipline-Specific Guides

Every discipline has specialized resources. The Clearinghouse for Subject-Oriented Internet Resource Guides, a joint effort of the University of Michigan's University Library and School of Information and Library Studies, offers guides to resources on the Internet for roughly 200 subject areas, from statistics to women's health resources, job hunting to alternative medicine. A Gopher version (*gopher://gopher.lib.umich.edu*) and a slightly abridged hypertext version (*http://www.lib.umich.edu/chhome.html*) are available. The guides often run 20 to 30 pages.

Alternatively, you can create your own discipline-specific guide by running a search program on a general topic, as you might with a Yahoo search on biology

http://www.yahoo.com/Science/Biology

Guides such as these can be invaluable sources of addresses, as well as of clickable links, for further investigation.

Key-Word Search Programs

When you have no idea where to start, you might turn to a key-word search program. This solution, however, is not as surefire as it might first appear.

Key-word search programs are useful for finding unique names of persons or places (proper nouns) or specific terminology for which there would be no likely synonym. They are not as useful for general terms for which there might be a plethora of resources.

Once you decide that a key-word search is appropriate, other decisions must be made. You must choose a particular search program and, with that, what to search and how.

Major key-word search programs include:

eXcite

http://www.excite.com

DEC AltaVista

http://www.altavista.digital.com

Yahoo Search

http://www.yahoo.com

Lycos Search

http://lycos.cs.cmu.edu

New search programs are constantly appearing. An up-to-date list can always be obtained at *http://www.yahoo.com/ computers_and_internet/internet/world_wide_web/searching _the_web/ search_Engines/* or *http://rs.internic.net/scout/toolkit/search.html.*

No single search program searches all of the Internet. Different search programs search different databases, or search the same ones differently. Some search titles or headers of documents, others search the documents themselves, still others search other indexes or directories. Some search the URLs describing the location of a text, others the URLs embedded within hypertext pages. Finally, some search programs also search other databases, such as Gopher listings. (See "Web search tool features," *http://www.unn.ac.uk/ features.htm* and Understanding WWW Search Tools, *http://www.indiana.edu/~librcsd/search/*)

Sites such as the MetaCrawler Multi-Threaded Web Search Service (*http://metacrawler.cs.washington.edu:8080/index.html*) offer simultaneous searching of a variety of search programs, while sites such as RES-Links: The All-in-One Resource Page (*http://www.cam.org/~intsci/*) offer links to a wide variety of search engines covering all aspects of the Internet, not only the World Wide Web.

The sheer number of citations returned need not be the major concern. A large number of "hits" from mailing list correspondence may not be that productive. Again, your research must be guided by knowledge and reflection.

Glossary

Anonymous FTP A file retrieval program with a common public password. *See also* File Transfer Protocol.

Archie A search program providing listings of the locations of files available by anonymous FTP. Also the automated indexing program upon which such searches are based.

Archive (verb) To combine two or more files into one.

Archive site A computer that stores and provides access to a specific collection of files.

ASCII file A file encoding format, developed by the American Standard Code for Information Interchange, that represents upper- and lowercase letters, numbers, punctuation marks, and basic operations (for example, tab, enter) by numbers from 1 to 128. A file encoded in standard keyboard characters—as opposed to a binary file. An unformatted text file. *See also* Binary file.

Binary Represented by ones and zeros, for example, 11001001.

Binary file A file encoded in binary code. More often, a file encoded with characters including but not limited to those found on a standard keyboard. Executable programs are stored as binary or nontext files.

Bit (binary digit) A single unit of data.

Browser Specifically, a program for reading the Hypertext Markup Language of World Wide Web pages. More generally, any program for following a path of menu items or other links.

Bulletin board system (BBS) An on-line computer network offering information and messages. Generally nonprofit and local or interest-group focused. *See also* On-line service.

Byte Eight bits. The number of bits necessary to indicate a single number or letter of the alphabet.

Chat A program or forum for on-line group discussion.

Client A computer system, program, or user that requests services from another computer, the server, on a network. *See also* Server.

Compression The reduction in the size of a file to achieve a smaller storage space or faster transmission.

Cyberspace The electronic world of computers and their users. The conglomerate information and resources of the Internet and other networked communication services.

Database Any collection of data or interrelated files that can be accessed in a variety of ways.

Decode To convert an encoded file back to its original form. *See also* Encode.

Digital Generally, using numbers or other discrete units—as with a digital, as opposed to analog, watch. The term is synonymous with any binary–coded system or device, hence essentially synonymous with *computer.*

Directory An index of the location of files, as on a hard drive of a computer. Directories create the illusion of file drawers, even though the files may be physically dispersed.

Discussion Group A forum in which subscribers communicate by exchanging group E-mail messages.

Domain A portion of the hierarchical system used for identifying Internet addresses. Key domains include: .COM (commercial), .EDU (educational), .NET (network operations), .GOV (government), and .MIL (military).

Domain Name System (DNS) The system for translating alphabetic computer addresses into numerical addresses.

Download To receive information or files from a remote computer.

E-mail Electronic mail.

Electronic texts   Texts encoded for electronic storage or transmission.

Emoticon   A symbol used to indicate emotion or the equivalent of a voice inflection in an E-mail message. *See also* Smiley.

Encode   To convert a file from one format to another, as from binary to ASCII for E-mail transmission.

Encryption   The coding of data for purposes of secrecy and/or security.

Extension   An abbreviation (usually three-digit) added to file names to indicate the file format.

FAQ   *See* Frequently asked question.

File   Stored computer data representing text, numeric, sound, or graphic images.

File transfer protocol (FTP)   A program for transferring files from one computer (a host) to another (a client), especially for retrieving files from public archives. *See also* Anonymous FTP.

Frequently asked question (FAQ)   A common name for files compiling answers to common questions, hence providing introductory information on a topic. Often appearing in newsgroups.

FTP   *See* File transfer protocol.

Gateway   A device, program, or site providing access to a network, generally between otherwise incompatible formats or protocols.

Gopher   A hierarchical menu program for accessing information across the Internet.

Gopherspace   That part of the Internet accessible by Gopher, that is, on Gopher servers and listed in Gopher menus.

Graphic interface   A computer interface that displays graphic elements and icons rather than only lines of simple text. A computer interface negotiated with a mouse as well as with cursor keys.

Home page   An initial menu page of a World Wide Web site, written in Hypertext Markup Language (HTML).

Host   A computer that allows other computers to communicate with it.

Hypertext Markup Language (HTML)   The system of embedding retrieval commands and associated addresses within a text; used for documents on the World Wide Web.

Hypertext Transfer Protocol (HTTP)   The program controlling the transmission of documents and other files over the World Wide Web.

Hytelnet A menu-driven version of telnet. A menu of telnet sites.

Icon A graphical representation or symbol representing a file, program, or command on graphic-interface programs.

Interface The connection between two devices. More particularly, the nature of the display screen used for communication between user and computer.

Internet The worldwide "network of networks" connected to each other using the Internet protocol and other similar protocols. The Internet provides file transfer, remote login, electronic mail, and other services.

Internet Protocol (IP) A protocol involving packets of data traversing multiple networks. The protocol on which the Internet is based.

Internet Service Provider A national or local company providing access to the Internet.

Internet Society (ISOC) A nonprofit, professional membership organization that sets Internet policy and promotes its use through forums and the collaboration of members.

IP *See* Internet Protocol.

IP address The 32-bit address, defined by the Internet Protocol and represented in dotted decimal notation, cf.

171.292.292.23, assigned to a computer on a TCP/IP network.

Jughead (Jonzy's Universal Gopher Hierarchy Excavation and Display) A variant of Veronica that searches directories on a select number of Gophers.

Key-word search program A program for searching a database or set of files for a specific term or terms.

Listserv One of a number of listserver programs.

Listserver An automated mailing list distribution program providing the basis of many mailing list subscription or discussion groups.

Logoff To relinquish access to a computer network.

Logon To gain access to a remote computer or computer network.

Mailing list A system of forwarding messages to groups of people via E-mail.

Microsoft Windows A graphic-interface operating system from Microsoft Corporation for IBM-compatible computers.

Modem (Modulate/Demodulate) A device that enables computers to transmit and receive information over telephone lines by converting between digital and analog signals.

Mosaic   The initial World Wide Web browser program.

Multimedia   Integrating text, sound, and graphics.

Netiquette   Proper social behavior on a network.

Netscape   A leading World Wide Web browser program.

Network   A communication system consisting of two or more computers or other devices.

Network Information Centers (NICs)   Organizations providing documentation, guidance, advice, and assistance for a specific network.

Ntalk   New talk, a new form of talk program. *See also* Talk.

On Ramp   *See* Gateway.

On-line service   A centralized computer network offering subscribers a variety of services including E-mail, file transfers, chat groups, and business, entertainment, and educational materials. Any service accessed by telephone.

Operating system   The primary program of a computer, cf. MS-DOS, Windows, Macintosh System 7. The operating system determines the basic commands and the appearance of the screen.

Prompt   A message or signal in a computer program requesting action by the user.

Protocol   A formal description of operating rules.

Search program   Any program providing direct examination of a database.

Server   A host computer serving a special function or offering resources for client computers, whether as a storage device in a local area network or as a Gopher site on the Internet.

Shareware   Commercial software available initially free on a trial basis.

Smiley   An icon used to convey emotion or innuendo in texts, e.g., :-) (glad), :-[(disappointment).

Spamming   Deluging someone with unwanted messages as punishment for inappropriate use of an on-line service or the Internet.

Surfing   Random or otherwise seemingly undirected browsing, as of the World Wide Web.

Talk   A program in which two users exchange on-screen messages.

Telnet   An Internet program for accessing remote computers.

Text interface   A screen display limited to lines of keyboard characters.

Uniform resource locator (URL)   A format for indicating the protocol and address for accessing information on the Internet; a name identifying documents and services on the Internet.

Unix   A popular operating system important in the development of the Internet.

Upload   To send files to a remote computer.

URL   *See* Uniform resource locator.

Usenet   A network and program for reading and posting messages on public newsgroups; accessible in whole or in part via the Internet or many on-line services.

Veronica(Very Easy Rodent-Oriented Net-Wide Index of Computerized Archives)   A program developed at the University of Nevada at Reno in late 1992 for searching Gopher menus.

Wide Area Information Server (WAIS)   A program for searching collections of documents for specific terms.

Word processor   A computer program that replaces all the operations formerly associated with a typewriter.

World Wide Web (WWW) A hypertext-based system for finding and accessing Internet resources.

SECTION TWO

Educational Research on the World Wide Web

6

The Internet contains a vast reservoir of outstanding educational sites. You no longer need to wait your turn at the local library to get information because you have the resources of the Internet at your fingertips. It is a simple matter to visit the Louvre Museum, which has an online exhibition of the museum's most celebrated artwork. When you surf the Net, you can find an analysis and discussion of the works of Shakespeare, visit NASA and find spectacular satellite photos of outer space. Furthermore, you can visit virtually any country in the world and find out more about its history and culture. You can access the latest weather reports worldwide, find lesson plans on any subject, get any statistic you need for your research report, and obtain historical information on famous mathematicians. However, to avail yourself of these treasures, you have to learn how to find your way around the Internet.

SEARCH ENGINES

When you search on the Internet you must realize that everything is constantly changing, because the Internet is growing at a phenomenal rate. To find the exact information you want, requires searching strategies. Fortunately, the Web (The Internet's graphical interface) has good locators called search engines that help find information. In the past three years, the search engines have increased in number and become more sophisticated and complex. They bear names such as Infoseek, Alta Vista, Lycos, Web Crawler, DejaNews, and Yahoo. Each search engine yields slightly different results depending on their focus and comprehensiveness. Some give full-text searches of the Web page, others group sites together, while others search for keywords in links that are present. Other tools focus on specific types of Internet material, such as FTP software sites or newsgroups archives. If one search engine doesn't provide you with the necessary information try another. Note, when you find one or two favorite search engines add them to your browser's bookmarks.

As you can surmise, search engines are invaluable tools in helping you manage the Internet. Because of their importance, it is necessary to learn how to use them in an efficient and skillful manner. There are some general tips for searching that will help you find the information you need thus avoiding the hassles of unfruitful searches.

Tips for Searching

1. Restrict your search by typing in the appropriate keywords. For example, you might specifically search for "Pandas" as a subject. Typing this name eliminates other references to other animals. What you type in the search box can be thought of as the answer to the question "What sites are available on Pandas?"

2. However, if your search term is too narrow, you may need to broaden it to find a larger selection of sites. For example, if you are looking for something on the Atlanta Braves, it would be wiser to look for the broadest category sports and then narrow it down to professional sports and then still limit it to major league baseball and finally your target the Atlanta Braves. Using this procedure, you get a wider selection of sites for the Atlanta Braves.

3. Know the different resources that can help you find your way around the Internet. For a starting point two valuable resources are *Xxplore* and *Yanoff's Internet Services List*. *Xplore* is a Guide to the Web that has organized sites into subject categories such as art, music business, education, sports. Its URL is:

    http://www.xplore.com/xplore500/medium/menu.html

    Additionally, *Yanoff's Internet Services List* offers a handy encyclopedia to hundreds of sites. The URL is:

    http://www.spectracom.com/islist/

FIGURE 1   *Xplore*
http://www.explore.com/xplore500/medium/menu.html

FIGURE 2   *Yanoff's Internet Services List*
http://www.spectracom.com/islist/

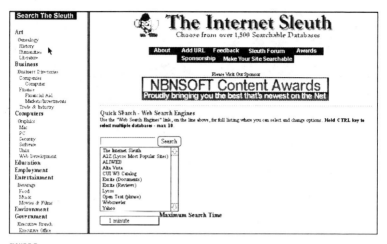

FIGURE 3 *Internet Sleuth*
http://www.isleuth.com/

4. Although there is an enormous amount of information on the Internet not everything is free. For example, the *Encyclopedia Britannica* gives you a free trial period then you must pay an access fee.

5. In previous paragraphs, we have mentioned four or five different search engines for the Web. Besides these sites, there is an easy way to access a greater variety of search engines. By using Web pages dedicated to multiple search engines, you can see the rich array of tools that are available such as *All-In-One Search* and *Internet Sleuth.*

   All-in-One Search **http://www.albany.net/allinone/** features a compilation of various search tools to help you find things on the Internet. If you scroll down the page and click on World Wide Web you will find *Alta Vista Web Search, Infoseek, Lycos,* and other search tools. Another Web page dedicated to listing and working with search engines is *Internet Sleuth* **http://www.isleuth.com/** This site provides a quick key word search of over 1000 searchable databases on the Internet. Enter a key word in one of the following search tools: Lycos, Infoseek, Alta Vista to find list of Internet sites that may contain the requested information. You can also search the *Internet Sleuth* by category.

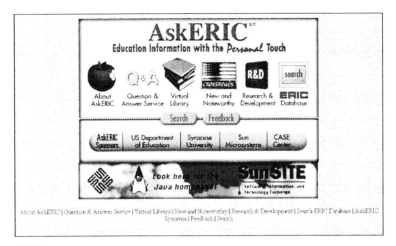

FIGURE 4 *AskERIC Virtual Library*
http://ericir.syr.edu/

6. Another excellent resource on the Internet is other people. If you are searching for a piece of information, sometimes people on listserver or in a newsgroup can help you with your search. The Frequently Asked Questions section (FAQ) of some discussion groups are very useful. In conclusion, there are many other searching tips, but this should provide you with a starting point for your explorations of the Web.

EDUCATION WEB LINKS

There are number of Web sites that provide educational resources for K-12. Three award winning sites are *AskERIC Virtual Library*, *Kathy Schrock's Guide for Educators* and the *NASA Space Link*.

AskERIC Virtual Library contains hundreds of lesson plans in all subject areas, satellite photos, and links to many other educational resources.

http://ericir.syr.edu/

Kathy Schrock's Guide for Educators is a huge inventory of web sites arranged in categories.

http://www.capecod.net/Wixon/wixon.htm

FIGURE 5 *Kathy Schrock's Guide for Educators*
http://www.capecod.net/Wixon/wixon.htm

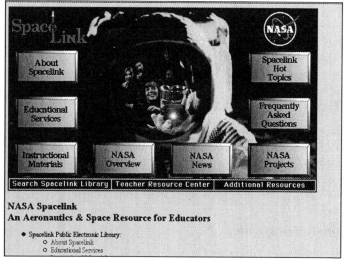

FIGURE 6 *NASA Space Link*
http://spacelink.msfc.nasa.gov/

Finally, *NASA Space Link* is an excellent resource for science information and classroom projects.

http://spacelink.msfc.nasa.gov/

EDUCATION, THE INTERNET, AND THE FUTURE

The World Wide Web has certainly provided educators with a vast library of resources. It is important for faculty and students to use the searching tools wisely and develop techniques for surfing the Web in order to find out what is available. In the last five years using document searches as waned in favor of online searches. Instead of searching libraries for relevant articles, it has become popular to electronically search the Internet. For instance, there are more publications such as the *National Science Teachers Association* NSTA online **http://www.nsta.org/** and *The National Council for Social Studies* (NCSS) **http://www.ncss.org/** NSTA is a leading professional organization for improving the teaching of science in grades K-12. The site features information about sponsored publications, programs projects and provides links to numerous online resources. NCSS is a leading professional organization for K-12 social studies teachers. This site includes teaching resources, professional development activities, online publications, news and other Internet Resources. Teachers can subscribe to a listserv mailing list for sharing their ideas via e-mail.

As a result of the Internet, much of the research process can transpire from the desktop which saves time and makes searches more efficient and successful. Nevertheless, there are still problems with the Internet. The access time is very slow and we envision this problem being solved in the near future. Security is becoming a real issue as the number of unscrupulous individuals on the Net multiply. There also is a real concern about copyright and authorship of the pages on the Net. Furthermore, there is a fine line between the right to free speech and the abuse of this right. Parents are concerned about sites that are not appropriate for their children and dangerous individuals that could lurk behind false identities. In the near future, these problems and issues will have to be resolved. Nevertheless, the Internet is a very exciting and stimulating place for educational research for students and faculty. It is by experimenting and surfing the Net that you will improve your searching skills. We know the experience can be overwhelming so don't be discouraged. You will learn quickly what will work and not be successful. Keep careful notes of your techniques and bookmark the search engines that you find useful. After you become a frequent user, you will be surfing the web and finding information that you never dreamed existed. Good Luck on your Internet Journey!

Internet Exercises by Topic   7

INTRODUCTION TO EDUCATION

1. Using a search engine, enter the name of an influential educational theorist to find a list of Web sites. For example, you might enter the name of John Dewey. This results in a Dewey John link with a list of resources about this philosopher of education. At this site you see biographical information on Dewey. If you click on one of the links under "Descriptions of Books About John Dewey", you find a description of that book. Other links give you the complete text version of specific Dewey work. For general information on Dewey, you can click on the "Center of Dewey Studies." You can see Dewey's legacy by clicking on either "University of Chicago's Laboratory schools" or "University of Michigan's School of Education's Dewey's Web."

    Next, enter the name of an important educational theorist, such as Jean Piaget, Plato, Rousseau, Alexander J. Inglis, Herbert Spencer, John Heinrich Pestalozzi. Can you find research or journals that are based on their work? Which theorists are more widely referenced? Is this evidence of their contribution to Education?

2. Enter key concepts from a major educational theorist in your search engine. For example, type in the "forgetting curve." What sites did you find that had nothing to do with educational psy-

chology? For instance, you may find a link that refers to restructuring plans. Were there relevant sites that referred to Hermann Ebbinghaus series of studies on the characteristics of memory?

3. Enter "Phonics" into a search engine. What type of results did you find? Can you find any research that the phonics approach produces better results, in reading comprehension than other approaches. What other topics did you find on these pages? How do these issues relate to phonics. How can we use phonics to improve student's reading?

4. Enter the key word "ESL" into a search engine. What type of results did you find?

Tips for Searching

Search engines like Yahoo let you search by general categories such as education. Within the category you want, enter a keyword to delimit your search. Once you exhaust the possibilities in Yahoo continue your search in Alta Vista, a more powerful search engine.

THEORIES/METHODOLOGIES

5. Using a search engine, find the *National Council of Mathematics* (NCTM) home page. At this Web page, find information on the journals that the NCTM sponsors. What is the emphasis in terms of theory , methods or issues in these journals? What journals are at your university ? Read through the recent issues of these particular publications and see what techniques and research methodologies the articles use. Are there any particular trends? Do you see one methodology emphasized more than another?

6. *School Library Hotspots* contains a vast variety of resources for education students. The URL is:

   **http://www.mbnet.mb.ca/%7Emstimson/text/
   hotspots.html#REFERENCE**

   Under Hotspots References, can you find the Clearinghouse for Subject Oriented Internet Resources (Argus Clearinghouse)? Were you amazed at the number of links there?

7. There are a number of research centers with Web pages. Using a search engine, locate some of these organizations. For exam-

ple, some well known ones are: *Educational Research Information Center ERIC* and other Clearinghouses including *ERIC Clearinghouse on Assessment and Evaluation, ERIC Clearinghouse on Elementary and Early Childhood Education, ERIC Clearinghouse on Science, Math and Environmental Education (ERIC/CSMEE),* and *ERIC Clearinghouse for Social Studies/ Social Science Education (ERIC/ChESS).* Some other major research centers are: the *Eisenhower National Clearinghouse for Math and Science, National Research and Development Centers Regional Educational Laboratories, Star Schools Program Sites, Comprehensive Regional Assistance Centers, US Department of Education,* and the *Association for Supervision and Curriculum Development (ASCD).* What kind of reports and information do you find? What are the different specialties of the ERIC centers?

8.   The student can find a wide range of online educational journals from the *Educational Journal Annotations.*

   http://www.soemadison.wisc.edu/IMC/Intedres.html

   This journal is a comprehensive annotative listing of the major journals with a link to their respective sites.

9.   Educators use other sources for data including newsgroups and listservs or mailing lists. What types of information are discussed in these groups? Can you find articles or discussions on class size, math reform, special needs, learning experiences for the disabled, technology education, literacy?

Tips for Searching

If you find a site that is relevant, such as gifted education, delve into the site and look for related links that could provide more information on your topic.

   Over 10,000 government documents can be retrieved via the *FedOnline* system. The *SunSITE Archives* at the University of North Carolina System is the best source for full text of important new government reports. The *Regional Educational Laboratories* **http://www.nwrel.org/national/regional-labs.html** are educational research and development organizations supported by U.S. Education Department, Office of Educational Research and improvement(OER). These ten labs offer resources to the schools in their local areas.

CURRICULUM AND INSTRUCTION

Art

The Web is a rich resource of art treasures, art news and curriculum materials for teachers and students. One of the best resources for art teachers is the *Kennedy Center's ArtsEdge*. Use a search engine to find this site which contains curriculum examples, goals and standards for art education, and links to curriculum assessment sites.

10. Use a search engine to find the ERIC Art Gopher menu which features hundreds of free lesson plans and resources for art educators. There are lessons on art appreciation, mask making, famous artists and much more. Again, use your search engine to find the site "Favorite Lessons." Did you find any lessons that you could use in your teaching? Do you have a favorite lesson that you would like to submit at this site? Peruse "Favorite Lessons" and locate its home page where you will find other art resources.

11. Use a search engine to find the *Getty Museum*. At this site, you will find lesson plans, resources, and online exhibitions, presented by the Getty Center for Education in the Arts.

Tips for Searching

If you want to find a nice collection of Art resources for K-12 go to *Web Sites and Resources* the art page whose URL is:

http://www.csun.edu/~vceed009/art.html

12. In searching the Web, find interesting sites that illustrate techniques for creating art projects. For example, visit Origami sites and learn how to create three-dimensional paper art. Were you able to find the sites *Fascination Folds Jasper's Guide for Paper Folding Instructions on the Web*, and *Joseph Wu's Origami Page*? Were you able to find other sites that teach visual arts, and painting techniques?

13. There are a plethora of art museums on the Web where students and teachers can analyze and study different artists and paintings. They can virtually travel to different cities such as Paris, Moscow and Florence and see their famous museums. Using your search engine, visit the Louvre and examine the Mona Lisa. What other exhibits and artwork did you visit at this museum? Take another virtual tour by visiting, *Treasures of the Czar*, which features more than 250 art treasures from the reign

of the Romanov czars 1613-1917. Visit the *Uffizi Gallery* containing an online collection of some of the most famous painting from the 14th-18th centuries.

14. Use a search engine to find places where students can post their art work on the Web. Three excellent examples are: *Art Space,* an online high school gallery, The *Visa Olympics of Imagination,* a contest for students 11-13 to draw or paint their own Olympic Sport of the future, and *Global Show-n-Tell Museum* where children of all ages can exhibit their art.

Treasures of the Louvre is an online exhibition of the most celebrated artwork. *The World Wide Art Resource*s is a comprehensive registry of art museums, galleries and exhibits, located throughout the world. To locate art museums world-wide visit *Museums from A to Z.* Use Yahoo to find biographical information on famous painters.

BILINGUAL/ESL

15. Using a search engine, you can locate lesson plans, activities and resources that focus on Bilingual and ESL education. For example, locate *Paso Partners Bilingual Lesson Plans,* a site containing English and Spanish lesson plans in science and math. Another useful site is *Estrellita Accelerated Beginning Spanish Reading.* This page contains links to information or resources on the Net related to Bilingual Education.

16. Find Estrellita's main menu. What did you find out when you read the Newspaper Article on Estrellita? Visit the *Primary Education (K-3) Resources For Bilingual Educators.* What activities and resources did you find at this site? Using the Keywords "Bilingual Education Resources," find The *National Clearinghouse for Bilingual Education (NCBE).* This site contains an online library, language and education links, databases and links to publishers and distributors of bilingual education teaching materials. Were you able to subscribe to an e-mail news bulletin and an electronic discussion group at this site? By doing this, you are able to interact with teachers who teach children from diverse cultures.

17. Two other excellent language resources for Bilingual/ ESL are the *Center for the Study of Books in Spanish for Children and*

Adolescents and *Cuentos Infantiles*. Use your search engine, to find some interesting interactive online stories written in Spanish. As a starting point, search for stories written in Spanish by the famous author Ika Bremer. What stories did you find that you could share in class?

18. Can you find any illustrated fables written in Spanish for children? Use a search engine such as Alta Vista and find *Cuentos Infantiles*.

19. Using a search engine, find a site that has a schedule of workshops, names and addresses of publishers, bibliographies and recommended books in Spanish. First try the *The Center for the Study of books in Spanish for Children and Adolescents* then try *Mariuccia Iaconi Book Imports, Inc.*

Tips for Searching

If you want information about any Spanish speaking country in the world, use a search engine such as Alta Vista and enter "Spanish Speaking Countries."

20. Can you find ESL lesson plans contributed by teachers? Use your search engine to find "Teacher Tips" (from Gessler Publishing). Did you find the following activities: *Alphabet Matrix Activity* and *Dictionary Scattegories*?

21. Again utilize your search engine to find *Internet TESL Journal for Teachers of ESL*. What teaching techniques and projects did you find?

22. If you want to interact with other ESL instructors and ask questions about ESL search for *Dave's ESL Cafe on the Web*. Did you take Dave's ESL quiz or write on the ESL Graffiti Wall?

23. Using a search engine find *Teachers of English to Speakers of Other Languages* (TESOL). What kind of organization is this? Read an online research article from the TESOL Journal and the TESOL Quarterly? How would this influence your teaching of ESL students?

Visit TESL/TEFL Links for a large compendium of resources for the ESL teachers.

Foreign Language

24. What resources are available for foreign languages teachers on the Internet? Using a search engine find the *Human Languages Page*. Use a dictionary that helps you translate a word from a different language other than English. Are you able to find any language tutorials at this site? Can you find a list of college and universities with language programs? Is your college or university included on this list?

25. Can you find any general language resources for classroom activities, curriculum, syllabus design, and journals? Using a search engine, find *Foreign Language Teaching Foreign* (FL TEACH). Subscribe to a mailing list where you can ask a question about a topic, share an idea or a lesson plan or just read what your fellow teachers say. Messages will appear in your e-mail. Search the FL TEACH archives and read previous messages

26. Can you find a site to help elementary school kids learn about Japan and learn a few words in Japanese? For example, use a search engine to find *Kid's Window*. Is the site *Foreign Languages for Travelers* useful for learning some words in Japanese? Learn three new words in Japanese using their pronunciation guide.

Tips for Searching

When you use Infoseek search engine, avail yourself of the related topics on the left hand side of the page to find interesting sites. Many of the related sites have checks which indicate they were given a higher rating.

27. Where can I find names and addresses of places to study foreign language abroad? For example, use *Foreign Language Study Abroad for Teachers*

    http://www.csun.edu/~hcedu013/LanguageAbroad.html

    to find this information. Is there any other similar site that you found useful in your search?

28. Locate the *ERIC Clearinghouse for Language and Linguistics* and read two research publications. Do you agree with their major findings.

29. Using a search engine, find *Foreign Language Learning Center*. What did you find at the *Materials Resources Link*? Do you think this is an effective way to learn a foreign language?

Using Alta Vista, find the *Language 3 Initiative* home page. From there use the *Intercultural E-mail Classroom Connections* to seek partner classrooms for international and cross-cultural electronic mail.

GENERAL CURRICULUM ACTIVITIES TEACHERS

The Internet is a virtual goldmine for useful resources for teachers. Teachers from around the world have contributed to these selected resources which you can find by using the following sites.

30. WebEd K-12 Curriculum Links

    http://badger.state.wi.us/agencies/dpi/www/WebEd.html

    This pages covers such topics as history, politics, Early Childhood, College Career Information, Art Links etc. If you are interested in the current Presidential campaign you can find out what issues are involved that separate one party from another by visiting *Campaign96.*

31. Virtual Schoolhouse

    http://sunsite.unc.edu/cisco/schoolhouse.html

    Visit The Teachers' Lounge and find any resources that could be useful for teaching. Next, use The Schools and Universities on the Internet link and see if your school or University is listed.

32. KidLink

    http://www.kidlink.org

    KidLink is an international global networking project for middle school and high school kids. Join a networking project that would be of interest to you and your class.

33. Classroom Connect

    http://www.classroom.net

    Classroom Connect is a newsletter for K-12 classrooms where you can find lesson plans and a multitude of other educational resources. Visit *Jump Station* and click on GRADES–Global Resources And Educational Sites Index. Choose a topic such as Culture and locate three resources that would be useful to you.

34. Teacher Talk

    http://education.indiana.edu/cas/tt/tthmpg.html

    Teacher Talk is an online publication for secondary teachers which focus on current issues including sexuality, age, classroom management, cultural diversity and other related topics.

35. K-12 Kaleidoscope

   http://www.coreplus.calstate.edu/KALEIDO/Nav.html

   K-12 Kaleidoscope is a compendium of resources including current events, kid's sites, and much more. Use a Search or Reference Tool to find a site for math, language and science.

36. Pitsco Educational Technology Web Site

   http://pitsco.inter.net/pitsco

   Pitsco Educational Technology offers excellent Internet Resources for Teachers including Grant Information, Acceptable Use Policy Information and much more. If you click on Favorite links, you will find up-to-date information about Grants and Funding Check out the National Science Foundation and find out if the Grant Proposal Guide is useful. As a bonus use Ask an expert and Key Pals.

37. Web Sites and Resources for Teachers

   http://www.csun.edu/~vceed009/

   Web Sites and Resources for Teachers offers a huge collection of resources and lesson plans for K-12. Resources include creative classroom projects, interactive online activities, visits to museums and trips around the USA and other Countries. Visit a social studies museum and a science museum and find two resources that are useful to you. In math, play an interactive game and explain how this help teach logic to students.

38. Electric Library

   http://www.elibrary.com/

   Electric Library, updated daily, contains a variety of print material online including 150 newspapers, 900 magazines, and 2,000 works of literature. Select an online newspaper and explain how you would use it in your social studies teaching.

Tips for Searching

When you reach a site with useful metalinks, keep exploring other links in that site. If you are using Netscape 2.0 or higher as your browser, you can see where you have been under History menu.

LANGUAGE ARTS

Language Arts, is a subject area rich in resources including lesson plans, activities, references, children's literature, kid's Web publishing, and professional organizations,

39. Using your search engine, find *Web Resources for English Teachers*. This site contains a collection of lesson plans, poetry, reference sources, and discussion groups. Choose two language arts lesson plans and discuss ways you can use them in the classroom.

Tips for Searching

If you want to find a nice collection of language arts resources for K-12 go to *Web Sites and Resources* the language arts page whose URL is:

http://www.csun.edu/~vceed009/languagearts.html

40. Using Yahoo, select the category Education then enter the word Haiku. From the list of Haiku poetry sites choose a site that generates Haiku poetry and one that serves a Haiku tutorial. How do you integrate Haiku poetry into the language Arts curriculum?

same as above but enter Word Search Puzzles

In Yahoo the glasses connotate a superior site.

41. Again using Yahoo, select the Education Category, but this time enter "Word Search Puzzles." Select a word search site and create a word search puzzle. What kind of puzzles did you find at this site and are they useful in teaching Language Arts? Note an excellent word search site is John Potter's.

42. Using the search engine Yahoo, select References and then choose Dictionaries. Select the language you want and then select a dictionary. At the site enter the word penchant and then use the thesaurus. Try three other words on your own.

43. An additional two other great references sources are: *My Virtual Reference Desk* and *Bill's Library*. In *Bill's Library* in the Poet's Corner, read a poem by Walt Whitman. How could you make use of this resource in the language arts classroom?

An excellent reference source of dictionaries is the site *Research-It*.

44. The *Children's Literature Web Guide* is an excellent resource for children's literature. Using a search engine find it. At the site find three all-time best selling titles and share them with your

class. Furthermore, check out *Mark Twain Resources on the World Wide Web* for instructional materials.

45. Use a search engine find *I-Site Help page* and then select Aesop & Me. Select two fables to use with children and then discuss their moral implications.

46. A very interesting area for Language Arts is the opportunity of students to publish their writing on the Web. Using your search engine, again find *I-Site Help page* and then click on Book Nook. At this site, choose the grade level you plan to teach and then read three reviews. Do you plan to encourage your students to submit their reports to this site? Does this appear to be a wonderful motivational force for encouraging young authors? Another site that encourages student's writing is *KidPub WWW*. Select a story and evaluate it in terms of content, mechanics, and creativity.

47. Another interesting interactive site for student 4-12 is *Crayon*. This site enables the student to create his or her own newspaper on the Web. What sites would you choose to place in your newspaper?

For a collection of samples of kid's original works in language arts on the Web see *Kids Did This Hotlist*. If you want the ultimate kid's newspaper site check out *KidNews*.

48. Using your search engine, type in "NCTE" to find the National Council of Teachers of English. This is the leading professional organization for improving the teaching of English and Language Arts at all grade levels. Go to Teaching Ideas/Resources and select Research. Read a report on the latest findings on teaching written composition and discuss it in class.

MATH

Math is a fertile subject area for teachers and students on the Web. There are innumerable lesson plans, activities, online board games and links to professional organizations.

49. Using a search engine enter "math lesson plans" where you will find a list of sites containing these resources. Find *Blue Sky* and *ERIC lesson plans for math*. Hint: use the gopher menus to find the math subject area. Choose two plans from each gopher menu and implement them in the classroom.

Tips For Searching

You will find a wonderful collection of math sites by entering "Math Resources" in a search engine.

50. Using a search engine, type "MSTE" and you will find the home page for the *Office for Mathematics Science and Technology Education* at the University of Illinois. At this site select K-12 Mathematics Lessons. Use the database search to find Internet-related lesson plans. For example, you may want lesson plans for algebra in the middle school. How many lesson plans did you find?

51. Enter "Education Place" in a search engine and then select Math Center. Use Brain Teasers, Activity Search, and Math Links to find three challenging math activities.

52. Use the keyword "MEGA Mathematics" to find the site *This is Mega Mathematics!* Select a math topic, and write a review for that activity.

53. Using Yahoo, select Recreation and then type "Interactive Web Games." Choose "Recreation:Games:Internet Games:Interactive Web Games." Play a game on the Net. What would students learn from this game? Furthermore, using the search terms, "Zarf's List" you will find one of the best collections of interactive Web games.

The following sites are loaded with wonderful links to math sites.
Web Sites and Resources for Teachers Math Page
   http://www.csun.edu/~vceed009/math.html

and *Kathy Schrock's Math Page*
   http://www.capecod.net/Wixon/math.htm

and *Math Resources*
   http://www.stritch.edu/~math/resources.html.

54. Using a search engine, type in the words NCTM homepage. Select "Journals" and then decide which one is applicable to your teaching situation. Give your reasons.

55. Using a search engine, find *Eisenhower National Clearinghouse* (ENC). Visit the archives of The Digital Dozen and select five sites that you would like to place in your book marks. Explain how they were chosen.

56. Enter "Math Forum" in your search engine. Browse and search this site, the premiere math education resource on the Web. Visit What's New, Teacher's Place, and Steve's Dump and discuss

with the class what you find at each link. Another excellent site is *Yahoo's Math Education* site.

MUSIC

Music sites are not as prevalent on the Web for Education, but nevertheless there are some interesting sites.

56. Using a search engine, find *Music Educator's Home Page.* Under curriculum resources find two lessons that you could incorporates into the music classroom. What was unique about these lessons? Additionally, another good site is Children's Music List. Choose two links from this guide that are useful Web resources for a music teacher.

57. Using Yahoo, click on Entertainment. Next enter the word "composers" and click on composers. You will find a list of classical composers such as Bach, Beethoven and Mozart under Masters. Prepare a classroom presentation on a composer including biographical information and a description of some of his work.

58. Using Alta Vista as your search engine find *Music Education Online.* Choose Music Links and then select a couple of music organizations that you might want to join as a music educator. Why did you select those particular organizations?

59. Using a search engine, find *Schoolhouse Rock home page.* How would you integrate Schoolhouse Rocks's grammar and math into the curriculum. Do you think it would be useful in an elementary classroom? Why or why not?

SCIENCE

Science probably has the largest collection of sites on the Internet. In the education domain, there are lesson plans, activities, online museums, science education organizations and much more.

60. Using a search engine, locate *TEAMS Distance Learning.* At this site, select K-12 Lesson Plans. From this collection of lesson plans, choose one in life science, physics, and environmental education. Share you lesson plans with your classmates and develop a lesson plan library.

Tips for Searching

If you want to find a nice collection of Science resources for K-12 go to *Web Sites and Resources*, the science page whose URL is:

http://www.csun.edu/~vceed009/science.html

61. Another excellent lesson plan resource is Academy 1. Enter "Academy 1 Educational Projects" in your search engine. At the top choose Teacher then Curriculum Exchange. For your school level, select a lesson plan and demonstrate it in class.

62. Use a search engine to find *Frank Potter's Science Gems*. Choose a life or earth science activity for your grade level and present this activity to your class. What was their reaction and what did you learn from this experience?

63. Find *Blue Web'n Applications Library* on the Web. Go to the applications table and choose an activity, a project, a resource, and a reference site. Do you agree with their ratings? Which site is most useful to you?

64. Use a search engine to find *Kathy Schrock's Guide for Educators*. At this excellent resource, go to science & technology and find a site for animals, for geology, and for space/astronomy? How do you plan to use the activities in your teaching?.

65. Using your search engine, find *Science Learning Network*. Choose Science Learning Network Science Centers and pick two museum to visit. What did you find that you could share with your classmates.

66. Using Yahoo, enter "Science Museums and Exhibits." Visit a planetarium, and aquarium and a zoo. Which site would you like to revisit and why?

Two outstanding science sites for students are *Star Child* and the *Franklin Institute Science Museum*. At the Franklin online museum check out the inQuiry Almanack link.

67. Using your search engine visit, the *NSTA* site. Explore one of the online science journals. How can the information you learned from this journal help you in your teaching?

68. Using your search engine, visit the *NASA homepage*. Find three sites that you could use to teach your students about space exploration.

SOCIAL STUDIES

Social studies is also rich in Internet resources for teaching social studies. The resources include a compilation of lesson plans, activities, geography maps, online museums and professional organizations

69. Using your search engine, find *Celebrating our Nation's Diversity* which is a group of lesson plans designed by the U.S. Census Bureau built around diversity. Develop a mini-unit on teaching diversity at your grade level. Choose two lesson plans and use the pupil worksheets and handouts.

70. A tremendous collection of lesson plans is found at *Ron MacKinnon's Educational Bookmarks* site. Use a search engine and enter "Ron MacKinnon's Educational Bookmarks." At this site under lesson plans search Big Sky and AskERIC for social studies activities. Could you find a lesson plan for teaching civics, U.S. government, and economics? What unique lesson plan idea did you discover that you could incorporate in your everyday teaching?

Tips for Searching

Another excellent lesson plan resource is *Academy 1*. Enter "Academy 1 Educational Projects" in your search engine and you will find over 200 lesson plans for social studies.

71. A resource for teaching geography skills is *What Do Maps Show?* Using a search engine, find "What Do Maps Show?" List three geography skills that are taught at this site. Another geography resource for the elementary school is *Mapmaker, Mapmaker, Make Me a Map*. Furthermore, if you want a list of other map resources on the Net use the search words "Map-Related Web Sites" to see a listing of sites rich in weather maps, state maps, historical maps, city maps etc. Click on City Net and find five new facts about any major city and incorporate this information in your teaching.

72. A fabulous site for creating street maps is found in Infoseek. At the top of Infoseek menu bar, click on *Fast Facts*. Go to *Street Maps* where you will find the necessary information for creating your street map. Choose three landmarks around any city in the U.S.A. and create maps. What are some other interesting ways of integrating this site into the social studies curriculum?

Find *Virtual Tourist II* using your search engine. At this site you will discover an electronic atlas which contains maps and useful information about any city or region worldwide.

73. Use the Alta Vista or Yahoo search engines to find *The Historical Text Archive.* You can find information on African Americans, Asia, women's history and much more. Choose a topic of interest and prepare a presentation on your research. Also visit the *Pedagogical Resources* and find lessons and materials that you can use in the classroom to promote multicultural understanding.

74. Use a search engine to find the *Congressional Email Directory.* Write a congressman or a senator about a critical educational concern. Additionally, if you want to become more informed about the 1996 presidential election find *Election '96.*

75. Using your search engine find *From Revolution to Reconstruction and What Happened Afterwards.* (American History: The American Revolution Project) Browse this interactive American History Textbook and find an original source and an article that you can use in your social studies program. Prepare a content list of the major items contained in this document and show your students how they can use it in their social studies research reports.

76. Use your search engine to find *Seven Wonders of the Ancient World, Splendors of Ancient Egypt*, the *Institute of Egyptian Art and Architecture* at the University of Memphis, and *Exploring Ancient World Cultures.* You can use other similar sites in planning your tour of Egypt or any ancient civilization. What information should you include in your travelogue?

77. Visit an online museum or exhibit to enrich your social studies curriculum. Enter "History Museums" in your search engine. Some award-winning museums or exhibits are: *Abraham Lincoln Online, Ancient Olympic Games Virtual Museum, Benjamin Franklin Glimpses of the Man, Betsy Ross House, Czars, The U.S. Holocaust Memorial Museum* and *Welcome to the Whitehouse.* Prepare a report on some of the artifacts and exhibits you were able to explore on your visit to this site.

For a larger collection of history museum sites are found at *Welcome to the World Wide Web* (WWW) whose URL is:

http://www.icom.org/vlmp/

78. The major professional organization for social studies is the *National Council for Social Studies.* Use the search term NCSS

Online to find this site. Subscribe to a listserv mailing list for sharing your ideas with other social studies teachers via email. What are the major publications of this organization?

Special Education

There are a variety of resources for special education including lesson plans, activities and professional organizations.

79. Using a search engine enter "Deaf Education" to find the *Council on the Education of the Deaf* site. When you reach the site, tell the purpose of this group? Choose Curriculum Materials to find a wide selection of lesson plans. Jot down some lesson plan ideas for teaching the deaf.

80. Use a search engine to find *FishNet*. This site is a gathering place for academically talented teenagers. Locate information about your favorite college by using the College Guide and discuss this college in class. Next read an article in *Edge* (an electronic magazine with original content) and discuss its contents with your classmates.

81. Use your search engine to find *Internet Resources for Special Educators*. This sites includes information for regular and special education teachers including lesson plans, disability information, disability law, mailing lists, and Internet search tools. Choose Disability Research and report on the finding of two studies. What implications does this have for teaching special education students?

82. Using the search term "NFB" find the *National Federation of the Blind* site. What is the purpose of the *National Federation of the Blind*? Name two leaders and give their contributions to the study of the blind.

83. Use a search engine to find *SERI*. The *Special Education Resources on the Internet* is a collection of Internet resources which may be of interest to those involved in the fields related to Special Education. Explain what Attention Deficit Disorder is and prepare a short report on it. What are some tips on handling these type of students?

84. Using a search engine find *Disability Web Sites*. At this site find the DigiBook Project and explain to your classmates the purpose of this project. Visit the *Science Education Math Project* and explain some of their programs, research and resources.

Tips for Searching

Using Yahoo, choose Education as a category. Next, type in the search term "Special Education" and you will find a tremendous list of sites.

Internet Sites for the Educator

8

URLs by Topic

ART

Artist Index
http://watt.emf.net/wm/paint/auth/

Arts:Art History:Artists
http://www.yahoo.com/Arts/Art_History/Artists/

ArtServe
http://rubens.anu.edu.au/

Camden Kid's Art Gallery
http://homer.louisville.edu:80/~mfpetr01/art_gallery/camdart.html

Claude Monet
http://www.columbia.edu/~jns16/monet_html/monet.html

Diego Rivera
http://www.diegorivera.com/diego_home_eng.html

Famous Paintings
http://www.paris.org.:80/Musees/Orsay/Collections/Paintings/

Favorite Lessons
http://www.in.net/~kenroar/lessons.html

Fridge Artz Gallery
http://www.go-interface.com/fridgeartz/gallery2.html

Getty's ArtsEdNet
http://www.artsednet.getty.edu/ArtsEdNet/

Global Show-n-Tell Museum
http://www.manymedia.com/show-n-tell/

Kennedy's Center ArtsEdge
http://artsedge.kennedy-center.org/

Leonardo da Vinci
http://www.leonardo.net/museum/main.html

Museums from A to Z
http://www.vol.it/UK/EN/ARTE/MuseumsfromAtoZ.html

Sistine Chapel
http://www.christusrex.org/www1/sistine/0-Tour.html

Smithsonian Photographs Online
http://photo2.si.edu/index.html

Treasures of the Czars
http://www.times.st-pete.fl.us/treasures/TC.Lobby.html

Treasures of the Louvre
http://www.paris.org/Musees/Louvre/Treasures/

Uffizi Gallery
http://www.televisual.it/uffizi/index.html

Vid Kids Lesson Plans
http://cmp1.ucr.edu/exhibitions/education/vidkids/lessons.html

WebMuseum, Paris
http://watt.emf.net/louvre/

World Art Treasures WWW Server
http://sgwww.epfl.ch/BERGER/index.html

World Wide Art Resources
http://www.concourse.com/wwar/default.html

BILINGUAL

Paso Partners Bilingual Lesson Plans for Grade K
http://gopher.sedl.org/scimath/pasopartners/pphome.html

Bilingual Education Resources
http://www.edb.utexas.edu/coe/depts/CI/bilingue/resources.html

Famous Hispanics in the World and History
http://www.clark.net/pub/jgbustam/famosos/famosos.html

DRAMA

Educational Theatre Association (ETA)
http://www.etassoc.org/eta-home.htm

Theatre Central
http://www.theatre-central.com/

ESL

Dave's ESL Cafe on the Web
http://www.pacificnet.net/~sperling/eslcafe.html

ERIC Gopher Menu of ESL Teaching Ideas
gopher://ericir.syr.edu:70/11/Clearinghouses/Adjuncts/
ACLE/Digests

GENERAL EDUCATIONAL RESOURCES

CEARCH: The Cisco Educational Archive
http://sunsite.unc.edu:80/cisco/web-arch.html

Curriculum Web
http://www.curriculumweb.com/curriculumweb/index.html

EdWeb
http://k12.cnidr.org:90/

Heinemann
http://www.reedbooks.com.au/heinemann/

History Data base Meta Page
http://www.directnet.com/history

Jan's Favorite K-12 Resources & Projects
http://badger.state.wi.us/agencies/dpi/www/jans_bkm.html

Sendit K-12 Resources
http://www.sendit.nodak.edu/sendit/resource.html

School.Net for Online Educational Sources
http://k12.school.net/

The World-Wide Web Virtual Library: Education
http://www.csu.edu.au/education/library.html

Web66
http://web66.coled.umn.edu/

Web Sites and Resources for Teachers
http:// www.csun.edu/~vceed009

FOREIGN LANGUAGE

Foreign Language Learning Center
http://gwis2.circ.gwu.edu/~ed220x/Languages/

Foreign Language Teaching Forum (FL TEACH).
http://www.cortland.edu/www_root/flteach/flteach.html#resources

Human-Languages Page
http://www.willamette.edu/~tjones/Language-Page.html

Kid's Window
http://kiku.stanford.edu/KIDS/kids_home.html

Transword Crossword Puzzles
ftp://ftp.dartmouth.edu/pub/LLTI-IALL/365german-news/
tw/index.htm

HEALTH EDUCATION/PHYSICAL EDUCATION

Adolescence Directory On-Line (ADOL)
http://education.indiana.edu/cas/adol/adol.html

Dole 5 A Day Homepage
http://www.dole5aday.com/

Fronske Center Health Education Page
http://www.nau.edu/~fronske/he.html

KidsHealth.Org
http://kidshealth.org/index2.html

TAHPERD (Texas Association of Health, Physical Education, Recreation and Dance)
http://www.tahperd.sfasu.edu/TAHPERD.html

JOURNALISM

KidNews
http://www.vsa.cape.com/~powens/Kidnews3.html

Yahoo's Index of Newspapers K-12
http://www.yahoo.com/News/Newspapers/K_12/

LANGUAGE ARTS

Aesop & Me
http://i-site.on.ca/Isite/Education/Aesop/

Anagram Insanity
http://Infobahn.COM/pages/anagram.html

Bill Henderson's Library
http://www.io.org/~jgcom/library.htm

Children's Literature Web Guide
http://www.ucalgary.ca/~dkbrown/index.html

COLUMBIA UNIVERSITY BARTLEBY LIBRARY
http://www.columbia.edu/acis/bartleby/

Complete Works of William Shakespeare
http://the-tech.mit.edu/Shakespeare/

CyberKids
http://www.woodwind.com:80/cyberkids

Fluency Through Fables
http://www.comenius.com/fable/

Granddad's Animal Alphabet Book
http://www.maui.com:80/~twright/animals/htmgran.html

Greeting Cards on WWW
http://www.yahoo.com/Entertainment/Humor__Jokes__and_Fun/
Greeting_Cards_on_WWW/

Houghton Mifflin's Invitations to Literacy
http://www.hmco.com/hmco/school/rdg/itl/index.html

John's Word Search Puzzles
http://www.neosoft.com/~jrpotter/puzzles.html

Kids Did This Hotlist: Language Arts
http://sln.fi.edu/tfi/hotlists/kid-lang.html

KidPub WWW
http://escrime.en-garde.com/kidpub/

Lewis Carroll Home Page Illustrated
http://www.cstone.net/library/alice/carroll.html

Mark Twain Resources on the World Wide Web
http://web.syr.edu/~fjzwick/twainwww.html

National Council of Teachers of English (NCTE)
http://marvin.clemson.edu/ncte/ncte.home.html

Purdue Online Writing Laboratory (OWL)
http://owl.trc.purdue.edu/

Tales of Wonder
http://www.ece.ucdavis.edu/~darsie/tales.html

Teaching Children's Literature
http://www.ucalgary.ca/~dkbrown/rteacher.html

Theodore Tugboat
http://www.cochran.com/theosite/story/Begin.html

Wacky Web Tales
http://www.hmco.com:80/hmco/school/tales/

Webster's Online Dictionary
http://c.gp.cs.cmu.edu:5103/prog/webster

Your Personalized Book
http://www.ot.com/cgi/kids/book

MATH

Activities Integrating Mathematics and Science (AIMS)
http://204.161.33.100/

Ask Mr. Math
http://www.localnet.com/~rseiden/mr_math/ask_mr_math.html

Biographies of Women Mathematicians
http://www.scottlan.edu/lriddle/women/women.html

Clever Games for Clever People
http://www.cs.uidaho.edu/~casey931/conway/games.html

Drake High School Math Department
http://marin.k12.ca.us/~sfdhs/math/math.html#topofpage

Eisenhower National Clearinghouse (ENC)
http://www.enc.org/

Eric's Treasure Trove of Mathematics
http://www.planetary.caltech.edu/~eww/math/math.html

Explorer Home Page
http://unite2.tisl.ukans.edu/

Geometry and the Imagination in Minneapolis
http://www.geom.umn.edu/docs/doyle/mpls/handouts/
handouts.html

Geometry Center
http://www.geom.umn.edu/

Geometry Forum: MathMagic
http://forum.swarthmore.edu/

Good News Bears Stock Market Project
http://www.ncsa.uiuc.edu/edu/RSE/RSEyellow/gnb.html

How Far Is It?
http://gs213.sp.cs.cmu.edu/prog/dist

Lemonade Stand on the Web
http://www.fn.net/~jmayans/lemonade/

MacTutor History of Mathematics Archive
http://www-groups.dcs.st-and.ac.uk/%7Ehistory/index.html

Mankala

http://touchstonegames.com/mankala.cgi

Math Comics and Cartoons

http://www.csun.edu/~hcmth014/comics.html

Math Forum

http://forum.swarthmore.edu/

National Council of Teachers of Mathematics (NCTM)

http://www.pbs.org/mathline/nctmhome.html

Pi Home Page

http://www.ncsa.uiuc.edu:80/edu/RSE/RSEorange/buttons.html

Pi-Search Page

http://www.aros.net/~angio/pi_stuff/piquery.html

Planet Earth Home Page

http://www.nosc.mil/planet_earth/info.html

Puzzle Archive

http://www.nova.edu/Inter-Links/puzzles.html

Susan Boone's Lesson Plans

http://www.cs.rice.edu/~sboone/Lessons/lptitle.html

Synergetics on the Web:3-D Geometry and the Visual Arts

http://www.teleport.com/~pdx4d/synhome.html

This is MEGA Math: Los Almos National Laboratory

http://www.c3.lanl.gov/mega-math/

U.S. Naval Directorate of Time

http://tycho.usno.navy.mil/time.html

World of Escher

http://www.texas.net/escher

MULTIDISCIPLINE LESSON PLANS

Academy One

http://www.nptn.org/cyber.serv/AOneP/internet.html

Ask ERIC Virtual Library

http://ericir.syr.edu/Virtual/

Big Sky Lesson Plans
http://libfind.unl.edu:2020/alpha/Big_Sky_Lesson_Plans.htm

Houghton Mifflin Activity Search
http://www.hmco.com/hmco/school/search/activity.html

Kathy Schrock's Guide for Educators
http://www.capecod.net/Wixon/wixon.htm

Teacher's Edition Online.
http://www.feist.com/~lshiney/index.html

U.S. Department of Education
http://www.ed.gov/

MUSIC

Children's Music List
http://www.cowboy.net/~mharper/Chmusiclist.html

Classical Music
http://weber.u.washington.edu/~sbode/classical.html

Internet Music Resource Guide
http://www.teleport.com/~celinec/music.shtml

Music Education Online
http://www.geocities.com/Athens/2405/index.html

Music Educator's Homepage
http://www.athenet.net/~wslow/

Resources for Music Educators
http://www.ed.uiuc.edu/music-ed/home.html

Schoolhouse Rock WWW Page
http://iquest.com/~bamafan/shr/

Yahoo Classical Composers
http://www.yahoo.com/Entertainment/Music/Genres/Classical/
Composers/

USENET NEWS GROUPS

EdWeb
http://k12.cnidr.org:90/

SCIENCE

Access Excellence
http://www.gene.com/ae/

An Inquirer's Guide To The Universe
http://sln.fi.edu/planets/planets.html

Bill Nye, the Science Guy
http://nyelabs.kcts.org/

Biological Sciences Resources
http://137.142.42.95/Biosciences.html

Chemistry Teaching Resources
http://rampages.onramp.net/~jaldr/chemtchr.html

Cloud Catalog
http://covis.atmos.uiuc.edu/guide/clouds/html/cloud.home.html

Comet Shoemaker-Levy Collision with Jupiter
http://www.jpl.nasa.gov/sl9/

Dem Dry Bones
http://www.cs.brown.edu/people/oa/Bin/skeleton.html

Earth & Sky Radio Series
http://www.earthsky.com/

EE Link: Environmental Education on the Internet
http://nceet.snre.umich.edu/

Electronic Zoo
http://netvet.wustl.edu/e-zoo.htm

Elementary Science This Month
http://www.mankato.msus.edu/ci/elem.sci.html

Energy Quest
http://www.energy.ca.gov/energy/education/eduhome.html

EnviroLink
http://www.envirolink.org/envirohome.html

Exploratorium Science Snackbook
http://www.exploratorium.edu/publications/Snackbook/Snackbook.html

Family Explorer
http://www.parentsplace.com/readroom/explorer/

Field Museum
http://www.bvis.uic.edu:80/museum/

Florida Aquarium
http://www.sptimes.com/aquarium/default.html

Franklin Institute Science Museum
http://sln.fi.edu/

Hands-On Science Centers Worldwide
http://www.cs.cmu.edu/~mwm/sci.html

Heart Preview Gallery
http://sln2.fi.edu/biosci/preview/heartpreview.html

Hubble Space Telescope (HST) Public Pictures
http://www.stsci.edu/EPA/Pictures.html

Liftoff
http://liftoff.msfc.nasa.gov/

MicroWorlds: Exploring the Structure of Materials
http://www.lbl.gov/MicroWorlds/index.html

Missouri Botancial Garden (MBG)
http://cissus.mobot.org/MBGnet/

NASA and The California Institute of Technology Jet Propulsion Laboratory (JPL)
http://www.jpl.nasa.gov/

NASA Goddard Space Flight Center (GSFC)
http://pao.gsfc.nasa.gov/gsfc.html

NASA Space Shuttle Web: Archives
http://shuttle.nasa.gov/

National Science Teachers Association (NSTA)
http://www.nsta.org/

National Space Science Data Center Photo Gallery (NSSDC)
http://nssdc.gsfc.nasa.gov/photo_gallery/

NPR's Science Friday-Kids Connection
http://www.npr.org/sfkids/

Online Educational Resources (HPCC)
http://quest.arc.nasa.gov/OER/

Optical Illusions
http://www.lainet.com/~ausbourn/

Periodic Table of Elements on the Internet
http://www.cetlink.net/~yinon/

Plotting Courses Through the Net
http://www.smplanet.com/internet.html

Project Galileo: Bringing Jupiter to Earth
http://www.jpl.nasa.gov/galileo/

Questacon Home Page
http://sunsite.anu.edu.au/Questacon/index.html

Rainforest Action Network (RAN)
http://www.ran.org/ran/

Safari Touch Tank
http://oberon.educ.sfu.ca/splash/tank.htm

Science Hobbyist
http://www.eskimo.com/~billb/

Sea World-Busch Gardens Homepage
http://www.bev.net/education/SeaWorld/homepage.html

Spaceborne Imaging Radar-C Education (SIR-CED)
http://ericir.syr.edu/Projects/NASA/nasa.html

Star Child
http://heasarc.gsfc.nasa.gov/docs/StarChild/StarChild.html

Students for the Exploration and Development of Space (SEDS) Home Page
http://www.seds.org/

Teacher's Guides
http://www.bev.net/education/SeaWorld/teachergui
des.html

Teacher Resource Center (TRC) Activities Catalog
http://www.lerc.nasa.gov/Other_Groups/K-12/TRC_activities.html

Thinking Fountain
http://www.sci.mus.mn.us/sln/

University of California at Irvine Science Education Programs (SEP)
http://chem.ps.uci.edu/~mtaagepe/SciEd/SEPmain.html

University of Tennessee Science Bytes
http://loki.ur.utk.edu/ut2Kids/science.html

Views of the Solar System
http://bang.lanl.gov/solarsys/

Volcano World
http://volcano.und.nodak.edu/

Weather Dude
http://www.nwlink.com/~wxdude/

Yahoo's Apollo Index.
http://www.yahoo.com/Science/Space/Missions/Apollo_Project/

Welcome to the Planets
http://stardust.jpl.nasa.gov/planets/

Welcome to The UC Museum of Paleontology (UCMP)
http://ucmp1.berkeley.edu/

Welcome to Quest!: Home of NASA's K-12 Internet Initiative
http://quest.arc.nasa.gov/

Welcome to WhaleNet
http://whale.simmons.edu/

You Can
http://www.nbn.com:80/youcan/

Yuckiest Site on the Internet
http://www.nj.com/yucky/about.html

SOCIAL STUDIES

African American History
http://www.msstate.edu/Archives/History/USA/Afro-Amer/afro.html

American Civil War Home Page
http://funnelweb.utcc.utk.edu/~hoemann/cwarhp.html

Ancient Olympic Games Virtual Museum
http://www.cs.dartmouth.edu:80/olympic/

Ancient World Web: Meta Index
http://atlantic.evsc.virginia.edu/julia/AW/meta.html

An Ongoing Voyage
http://sunsite.unc.edu/expo/1492.exhibit/Intro.html

Celebrating Our Nation's Diversity
http://www.census.gov/ftp/pub/edu/diversity/

Chinese Historical and Cultural Project (CHCP)
http://www.dnai.com/~rutledge/CHCP_home.html

CIA World Fact Book 1995
http://www.odci.gov/cia/publications/95fact/index.html

Congressional Email Directory
http://www.webslingerz.com/jhoffman/congress-email.html

Cybrary of the Holocaust
http://remember.org/

Electronic Fieldtrip to the United Nations
http://www.pbs.org/tal/un/

First Amendment Cyber-Tribune (FACT)
http://w3.trib.com/FACT/index.html

From Revolution to Reconstruction and What Happened Afterwards
http://grid.let.rug.nl/~welling/usa/revolution

History Channel
http://www.historychannel.com/index.html

Kings and Queens of Britain
http://www.ingress.com/~gail/

Lesson Plans and Resources for Social Studies Teachers
http://www.csun.edu/~hcedu013/index.html

Library of Congress Home Page
http://marvel.loc.gov/

National Clearinghouse for U.S.-Japan Studies
http://www.indiana.edu/~japan/

Martin Luther King Jr
http://webster.seatimes.com/mlk/index.html

MayaQuest '96
http://www.mecc.com/mayaquest.html

Migration to America: Ellis Island
http://www.turner.com/tesi/html/migration.html

Native American Indian
http://indy4.fdl.cc.mn.us/~isk/

Negro Leagues Baseball: 75 Years of Glory
http://www.infi.net/~moxie/nlb/nlb.html

Perry-Castañeda Library Map Collection
http://www.lib.utexas.edu/Libs/PCL/Map_collection/
Map_collection.html

Seven Wonders of the Ancient World
http://pharos.bu.edu/Egypt/Wonders/

Social Studies School Service
http://www.socialstudies.com/index.html

Speeches of the Presidents of the United States
http://www.ocean.ic.net/rafiles/pres/thelist.html

Splendors of Ancient Egypt
http://www.times.st-pete.fl.us/Egypt/Default.html

States: Government OnLine
http://www.asd.k12.ak.us/Andrews/States.html

Susan B. Anthony House
http://www.frontiernet.net/~lhurst/sbahouse/sbahome.htm

U.S. Census Bureau
http://www.census.gov/

U.S. Supreme Court Decisions
http://www.law.cornell.edu/supct/supct.table.html

Virtual Tourist II
http://wings.buffalo.edu/world/vt2/

Welcome To The White House
http://www.whitehouse.gov/

SPECIAL EDUCATION

Arc Home Page (a national organization on retardation)
http://TheArc.org/welcome.html

Disability Information and Resources
http://www.eskimo.com/~jlubin/

FishNet
http://www.jayi.com/sbi/Open.html

Vocational/Technical Education

Occupational Outlook Handbook
http://www.espan.com/docs/oohand.html

Technology Student Association (TSA)
http://www.tmn.com/Organizations/Iris/tsawww/tsa.html

For a listing of more than 700 award winning Educational Web sites, see *The Best Internet Sites for Teachers* by Vicki F. Sharp, Martin G. Levine and Richard M. Sharp, ISTE, 1996.